VOICES

OF

COLOR

The APPLAUSE Acting Series

VOICES OF COLOR

SCENES AND MONOLOGUES FROM THE BLACK AMERICAN THEATRE

Edited by
Woodie King, Jr.

An APPLAUSE original
Voices Of Color
Scenes and Monologues from the Black American Theatre

Copyright ©1994 by Applause Theatre Books

Library of Congress Cataloging-in-Publication Data

Voices of color : scenes and monologues from the Black
    American theatre / edited by Woodie King, Jr.
        p.   cm.
   ISBN 1-557853-174-2 : $9.95
   1. Acting.   2. Monologues. 3. Dialogues.
   4. American drama--Afro-American authors.
   5. Afro-Americans--Drama.   I. King, Woodie.
   PN2080.V65   1993
   812.008'0896073--dc20   93-33104
                                         CIP

British Library Cataloging-in-Publication Data
A catalogue record for this book is available from the British Library

APPLAUSE BOOKS
211 West 71st Street
New York, NY 10023
Phone: 212-595-4735
Fax: 212-721-2856

CONTENTS

Note: Brackets [ ] are inserted to indicate the speech of another character within a monologue or scene.

Note: The scenes and monologues included here may need to be adapted to the needs of your specific audition or class. As you think about making the necessary cuts, it is good to focus on what is important to you about the character and the dramatic action. When using material edited in such a manner, it is important to let your audience, class, or teacher know.

★

INTRODUCTION

The scenes and monologues presented here are taken from plays written by some of this country's finest playwrights. Black, White, or otherwise, they share a vision of the complex nature of Black identity in an evolving social milieu. The presentation of this nature is the job of today's (and tomorrow's) Black actor. The selections included in *Voices of Color* are intended to give Black students of acting both an important sampler of contemporary theatrical roles written for the Black actor as well as a source for material that relates directly to their own lives. Playing material that is intrinsically foreign to one's own identity is one of the greatest challenges that an actor faces. Attempting to study the craft of acting without unalienating material to work from can compound an already difficult process for the beginning actor. This is not to say that a Black actor should *only* perform Black material. It is, rather, to say that Black students of acting should be provided with material both by and for Black artists.

But, this book may serve a larger purpose, also. As America moves towards the new century, the theater is becoming a more segregated place. The very need to differentiate a "Black" professional theater from any other may be a sign of this backsliding tendency. Why is this happening? Black professionals who work in the Black theatre see these non-profit Black Theatres being systematically excluded from major funding; many see that funding going directly into White institutions. These White institutions set up training programs in acting for Black students. Many who work in the professional Black Theatre do not believe that these Euro-centric institutions have in hand the tools necessary to train the Black artist. Many of these institutions do not even have access to the materials that their Black students can relate to; students must use European or White American writers as role models. This alone certainly won't prepare students for work in the professional Black theatre. Materials written by Black playwrights must be included in the curriculum at this time. This book is a gathering place and a platform for the Black American voice as it makes itself heard in collegiate curriculums of inclusion, in the audition rooms of the major theaters of this nation, and in the annals of American literary history.

The list of living playwrights whose work is included here reads like a *Who's Who* of the American Theatre. They have all expressed a concern for the discipline of actor training, especially as it applies to the actors who will be interpreting their work: *Black* actors. These playwrights have made a lifelong commitment to Black culture by exploring it through their work. To the actor making a similar commitment, this book is dedicated.

Woodie King, Jr., 1993

Note: Brackets [ ] around a line of dialogue are inserted to indicate the speech of an additional character within a monologue or scene.

Note: The scenes and monologues included here may need to be adapted to the needs of your specific audition or class. As you think about making the necessary cuts, it is good to focus on what is important to you about the character and the dramatic action. When using material edited in such a manner, it is important to let your audience, class, or teacher know.

★

scene from
AS LONG AS LIFE LASTS
by Claudette Alexander-Thomason

About the play: This two-act surrealistic play has only three actors who become different characters throughout. They are the YOUNG GIRL, the WOMAN and the MAN. Most of the scenes are played center stage with the monologues played downstage right and left. The story is about the episodes which lead to the snatching and coming home (after nine years) of a four-year-old girl and how the characters cope with the uncertainty that these changes are bound to bring.

SCENE: The stage is bare except for a chair stage right and one stage left. Airport sounds can be heard as a young girl approaches a chair carrying only a small satchel. She is very agitated. She looks around and finally takes a seat.

YOUNG GIRL: Please Lord. Just help me get back to her. If you do this one thing for me, I ain't never gonna smoke or sneak no more Jack Daniels. Please, Lord. [*She looks around and spies the audience.*] Stop invading on my prayers. They are private you know. Well, if you just have to be nosy, I'll tell you what I'm praying about. Promise me you're gonna be quiet and listen 'cause if my stepmother has a notion that I'm here, she'll have my as-'cuse me-behind back home so quick, I'll see more stars than when I drink a whole bottle of JD. No, I ain't no drunk. I only drink when I'm alone with my dreams and my wishes and my mother. [*She laughs to herself.*] I guess you're confused right about now. [*She opens her satchel and presents a large picture of a woman.*] This is my mother. Ain't she gorgeous? My stepmother on the other hand is a dog's dog—in more ways than one. My Grandma says she have to tie a chicken bone 'round her neck for dogs to play with her. I don't know what she tied around her neck for my Daddy to play with, if she tied anything at all. I'm going home to see her—my real mother, that is if she still wants me or remembers me. [*In a conspiratorial whisper.*] I haven't seen her in nine years—well, ever since I came to live with my Daddy. He never lets me write her or call her or nothing. Always saying, "You ain't gonna be shit," "You just like your Momma, you little slut." What kind of way is that to talk to a child, your own daughter? That's what Grandma used to ask him and he'd tell her to mind her own damn business or she'd be on the streets peddlin' papers or prostitutin'. Ain't that awful? He was awful to me, the stepmadwoman, and especially to my Grandma. He didn't even have no friends. Well, he had one best friend—a fifth of Tangueray. That's gin for those of you who don't drink. [*Imitating a man.*] "I drink gin cause it ain't no sin." Yeah, right. That was the smallest sin he ever made, except me, maybe. How old am I? You won't believe me when I tell you. Everyone tells me I look older than sixteen. [*Pause.*] See, I knew you wouldn't believe me. I'm thirteen but I think like I'm twenty-nine. That's what Grandma says. I wonder what my real mother will say. [*She looks at her watch.*] Forty-five more minutes before we can even board. What I am gonna do? [*She looks around for a moment.*] I guess you've figured out by now that I'm runnin' away but it's more like I'm runnin' back. Only question is, back to what? [*Light slowly fades as the* **YOUNG GIRL** *sits. Lights come up on the* **WOMAN***. She is talking on the phone.*]

WOMAN: I know...I said I understand all of that. I just want to know when the plane is going to land in Seattle...You're gonna be there right? I mean on time....I'm sorry. Well after nine years what do you expect?...Alright, I'll try to be calm but it's so hard, sis. I can't thank you enough for this. If I live three lifetimes, I'll never be able to thank you enough. [*Starting to cry.*] Do you think she still loves me?...Yes, well, sure she's my daughter but it's been nine years and, well, we'll be like strangers and if I know the excuse for a man that is her biological father, he's lied through every tooth and cap in his mouth...Alright, I won't think about that. We've won, I know but that still doesn't stop the anger. I'm just counting the minutes until I can hold her in my arms again.

YOUNG GIRL and **WOMAN:** I wonder if she still loves me. [*The lights slowly fade on the* **WOMAN** *as she and the* **YOUNG GIRL** *simultaneously say "I wonder if she still loves me." Lights come up upstage center where the imagined reunion takes place. The two look at each other for a moment then the* **YOUNG GIRL** *runs into the* **WOMAN**'*s arms. They embrace and cry, look at* *each other, etc.*]

WOMAN: Oh, baby. Look at my baby.

YOUNG GIRL: Momma. Please don't let this be a dream. Please.

WOMAN: It isn't a dream. I'm here, I'll always be here. [*The* YOUNG GIRL *slowly pulls away and steps back.*]

YOUNG GIRL: But you weren't there when he did all those awful things to me, Momma. Why weren't you there?

WOMAN: It's a long story, baby. I think we should get you home and fed and then we'll talk.

YOUNG GIRL: You're so pretty, Momma. Is that why you didn't want me, because I looked like him and not you ?

WOMAN: No.

YOUNG GIRL: Then why?

WOMAN: We'll talk once you get settled in, darling. Now let's go get your bags.

YOUNG GIRL: Didn't my stepfather and sisters and brothers come to greet me or don't they want me either?

WOMAN: So many questions. At least your mind is still inquisitive. Just like when you were a little girl.

YOUNG GIRL: He said you were very educated. You and your whole family. He said that we wouldn't fit in. Do I fit in Momma?

WOMAN: We'll talk once we get you settled.

YOUNG GIRL: [*Defiantly.*] We'll talk now.

WOMAN: [*Impatiently.*] God help us and save us. You're just like him.

YOUNG GIRL: He said you never wanted me. That's why he took me.

WOMAN: It wasn't that way.

YOUNG GIRL: Why don't you tell me how it was, Momma? Or can't you think up a lie fast enough?

WOMAN: [*Slaps the* YOUNG GIRL.] I don't want you here. I'll buy you a ticket back.

YOUNG GIRL: I don't care. Nobody wants me anyway. She doesn't want me. [*They turn their backs to each other and start to walk to their places stage right/left.*]

WOMAN: She doesn't want me.

YOUNG GIRL: She doesn't love me.

WOMAN: She hates me. Nine years is a long time.

YOUNG GIRL: Where will I go?

WOMAN: What will I do?

YOUNG GIRL: No one loves me.

WOMAN: I love her. [*They sit in their places on stage, speaking to audience.*]

WOMAN and YOUNG GIRL: God, please let her love me. [*Black out.*]

★

scene from
JACK POT MELTING
by Amiri Baraka

Score should be a duet for violin and saxophone, each imitating the speech of the couples. Drums should open and close the play and the last words OK'd back and forth as a diversely spoken, plea, command, question, hope, prediction, confidence, struggle, as a final note of instruction and direction.

SCENE: BROTHER's apartment living room. There is a TV.

BROTHER: Glad to see you. [*Large head of Black man on TV turned on by* **BROTHER** *coming in room.*] Yes. [*Straightening, looking over shoulder.*] Glad you're there, dark in half darkness— I gotta get- [*Looks up- continues.*] You have to feel the connection. You have to be connected all right. [*Laughs. Turns on light.*] Where is that damn manuscript? You've got to see the right sun rising...is that how they say it? The right sun rising? [*Looks again suddenly at TV.*] Damn...that dude [*Stops, double takes.*] When did I do that? [*On the TV, a man speaks who looks and sounds just like* **BROTHER**.]

TV: Alright J.D., welcome to the gray nasty show, live from the stick's bottom. The wind is here standing, yes, the murder's eyes. The rattle of the various truths and lost chords.

BROTHER: [*Looks.*] What is this? Live? That me! [*Turns on another light.*]

TV: What is this? Don't light try to escape? Yes? But we knew older Ethiopians—Welcome. This is live. But first a word from our sponsor...[*Chains and whips with bells and jingles. Man jumps on phone, dials.*]

BROTHER: Hey! [*Lights come up on* **SISTER** *in another apartment.*]

SISTER: I was thinking about you. You s'posed to come by or I'm s'posed to come there?

BROTHER: Go turn on channel 2.

SISTER: What? What...?

BROTHER: Turn it on—Go hear—it's weird...

SISTER: [*She leans and turns on set. His image appears.*] What?

BROTHER: Yeh—You see that?

SISTER: When'd you do this?

BROTHER: I donno. But listen...

TV: OK, We're back. Inside the buttons on the leather furniture. With a harmonic and a steam engine. And our hot eyes. Even under the ocean. See the bubbles our hot eyes make...

SISTER: What?

BROTHER: Listen.

TV: Drink Crazy X! Eat Wild Z! Live. Yes, here we are *live*, under the monster's thumbnail. We're glad...

SISTER: What kind of joke...?

BROTHER: Whatever it is I ain't in it.

SISTER: Hey, if this is some TV trick, you can sue them.

BROTHER: Yeh, but, what's going on...

SISTER: Come on, call the station now—

TV: Glad the dust mote has spring to its dimensions. There is a life that's going to be here after the next message. The shadow the tip of the look, is alive we know. And so its future is thrilling and will be here soon. But first...

BROTHER: [*Phone.*] Hello! Yes, the program on your station, what is it? The Sidekick Show? Yeh—well who is that MC—what's he think he's doing? His name is what...Ben?

SISTER: Ben, Look at the TV—look?

TV MAN: [*A woman who looks and sounds just like* **SISTER** *appears on screen.*] Now my first guest this evening. I'm glad and she knows I'm glad as my footprint, the cube's gray sweat...

TV WOMAN: Yes! Glad would describe them. All my thrills of the corners to be turned! [*Throws up hands.*] Glad! Audience I am here with a sunbeam to speak of the love just around the next...[*They embrace.*]

BROTHER: [*To sis on phone.*] What crazy shit is this?

SISTER: I donno. What'd the TV people say?

BROTHER: They said it was me on the...that it was Ben—

SISTER: But the woman—who is that?

TV WOMAN: Yes, I'm Gloria. Black Wendy arrives post hamburger [*On TV they embrace, laughing.*] More! All? We...

TV MAN: We are glad to have such health for you. Such love zooming close. Just around the square concrete, and its excellent hard evils. The distance...

TV WOMAN: The granulated unmoving. Kept lingerings enshrined and shiny sometimes—We're Glad.

SISTER: [*On phone.*] What do you mean her name is Gloria. It's

why I'm calling. Because not only does the woman look like me—
and that guy like my boy friend, but they've got our names. [TV
MAN & WOMAN *singing a song—background, not clear, in
some harmony.*]

BROTHER: What are they telling you?

SISTER: They say that those are those people's real names and
that they're not made up. [*Now they both, still somewhat
dumbfounded, turn and look.*]

TV MAN & WOMAN: [*Sing.*] Iron is good to eat and steel and
glass and sand [*Terrifying unison.*] The fires are creeping up backs
and necks. The skeletons are tapping on the rain again! Open the
matches and collect your ransom, ignorance. We the dancing you.

BROTHER: Hey—this is too weird. I'll be over...[*A knock at
door.*]

SISTER: Yeh. I got a feeling...who is that [*Now a knock at her
door.*] Hey, I've got one too.

BROTHER: What ever is goin on it getting ice cold. [*Suddenly.*]
Hey, don't open that door.

SISTER: [*To door.*] Who is it? [*Dog starts growling and barking.
She is visibly shaken.*] My God it's some dogs...

BROTHER: Who's out there? [*Dogs are slowly building up their
vicious growling.*] They're dogs outside my door too. [*They look
toward TV.*]

TV MAN: Now its time for a visit from our best friends...Fame.
[*A little white puppy bounds on to the set.*]

TV WOMAN: & Fortune. [*A little puppy leaps out and into her
lap. They begin rocking them on TV like babies and serenading
them on and on.*]

TV MAN: Around the next corner—our lives are sweet like open windows.

TV WOMAN: We know every one's glad or I should say all of us...yes that a correction. All of us...that's in.

TV MAN: Yes, certainly, not every one—that's art.
[*Puppies yipping "yip, yip, yip" & etc.*] [*Dogs at B&S doors sound large and vicious—eager to attack!*]

BROTHER: This is not a joke—No trick VCR, right?

SISTER: I'm so frightened, I'm shaking.

BROTHER: What is going on?

TV MAN: You see at your door golden light from just around the corner.

TV WOMAN: [*A finger to her lips.*] Only say nothing...[*Instructions lightly.*]...and of course, remember nothing.

TV MAN: Right, say good-bye to lies! To old slow and the teeth.

TV WOMAN: Yes—glad you can do this. Help yourself. No help all us.

TV MAN: [*They're arrayed in proper home peaceful portrait now.*] Are you glad now? Are you watching?

BROTHER: [*To* SISTER.] We can't call anybody. I don't want us to get cut off.

SISTER: Who would you call?

BROTHER: Hey, we've got friends who'd help. People. Families.

SISTER: Why'd you leave that party early anyway? I was

looking for you...

BROTHER: Looking for me—You didn't seem like you were looking for me.

SISTER: God, Ben, you're a terrible male chauvinist. You can talk to any woman—its OK. But let any other brother pass a few innocent words and you come on like Darth Vader.

TV MAN: Be Glad! Be Glad!

TV WOMAN: Be there for each other!

BROTHER: Yeh, Why do I always get so uptight...

SISTER: Yeh. And I wish you'd stop it. Even if I wanted to go off with some beautiful man I have discipline...

BROTHER: Discipline? That's all that limits the drama to mouth play? Nothin' else?

SISTER: You mean you never see any woman you're not sexually attracted to...?

BROTHER: What?

SISTER: You now! Don't like—

BROTHER: But you're talking.

SISTER: What, you mean you can't stand to hear that I might find other men attractive. I had to get used to that with you immediately.

BROTHER: Yeh, but you said you knew that was just business.

SISTER: Yeh, until you had that affair.

BROTHER: Oh, Gloria, but that was a long time ago.

SISTER: I know! You're sorry

SISTER: OK, OK. [*They both look at each other, then turn to look at their two doubles who are now petting the dogs and crooning.*]

TV MAN: Fame.

TV WOMAN: Fortune. [*Then the brother and sister look at the door, the barking the snarling.*]

BROTHER: OK.

SISTER: OK.

[*Fade to black.*]

★

14

Monologue from
A MEDAL FOR WILLIE
by William Branch

William Branch has had a long and distinguished career in the arts and media fields. A graduate of Northwestern University, he holds a Master of Fine Arts degree from Columbia and did further graduate study at the Yale University School of Drama on a Yale-American Broadcasting Company Fellowship.

Winner of a John Simon Guggenheim Fellowship for creative writing in the drama, among his best-known works are *A Medal for Willie*, the play which launched his career when it was produced on a shoestring at a Harlem cabaret; *In Splendid Error*, an historical drama about Frederick Douglass and John Brown, which became an off-Broadway hit; and *A Wreath for Udomo*, based upon the novel by Peter Abrahams, which was prominently produced on the London stage.

A film and television writer-producer as well, Branch's media credits include *Light in the Southern Sky* for NBC, which won the Robert E. Sherwood Television Award; *Still A Brother: Inside the Negro Middle Class* for PBS, nominated for an Emmy and recipient of a Blue Ribbon Award at the American Film Festival; and *A Letter From Booker T.*, a PBS drama commissioned by its stars, Ossie Davis and Ruby Dee, which won a Citation from the National Conference of Christians and Jews.

Currently Professor of Theater and Communications at the African Studies and Research Center, Cornell University, Branch is editor/contributor of *Black Thunder: An Anthology of Contemporary African American Drama* (Mentor, 1992) and *Crosswinds: An Anthology of Black Dramatists in the Diaspora* (Indiana University Press, 1993).

SETTING: MRS. JACKSON is the mother of a Black American soldier killed in action. The stage of the auditorium of a Black high school in a Southern town following the presentation to Mrs. Jackson of her son's medal for bravery by a three-star general from Washington and local White officials. She has changed her mind and tries to give the medal back. They ask her why.

MRS. JACKSON: Why?

[**THE OTHERS:** Yes, why?]

MRS. JACKSON: All right, then. I'll tell you why. You asked me. Now I'm gonna tell you. [*She begins quietly and builds in intensity, a tower of strength and emotion.*] I didn't want to go through with this program an' all, to begin with. But standin' here just now, readin' off them words, I knew I just can't! I can't be that much of a hypocrite, not even for Willie. You-all 'spect me to 'cept this medal and read that speech you had all ready for me, say, "Thank you kindly, suhs," and then go home an' be happy about the whole thing. But I can't! I can't go through with this—this big LIE. [*The others are shocked.*] Yes, I said Lie. What has all your fine talk ever meant to Willie? He walked around this town nearly all his young life and nobody cared. You Jim-Crowed him and shunned him and you shoved him off in a corner. You gave him a third-rate schoolin' and when he wasn't quiet like a mouse, you put him out in the street. You looked down on him and you kept him down 'cause he was black and poor and didn't know no better than to believe that was the way things is supposed to be!

Yes, my Willie was dumb in a lotta ways. He didn't know nothin' 'bout no i-de-lol-logies or whatever you calls it. He wasn't fightin' 'cause he hated anybody. He joined the Army 'cause he couldn't get a decent job here. Willie thought if he did what they told him in the Army and didn't get in no trouble, maybe someday he could come back home and walk down the street and be somebody. Willie tried so hard, he got himself killed. But he didn't know. 'Cause even while you-all's here supposed to be honorin' Willie, you keep talkin' 'bout keepin' things the way they is. Willie didn't want things to stay the way they is. 'Cause it always meant he come out holdin' the short end of the stick—the Jim Crow end, the poor folks' end.

That's why this is all such a big lie. You-all here ain't really honorin' Willie. You here tryin' to tell yourself that you been *right* all along—that the way you been doin' things is perfectly okay 'cause you can get boys like Willie to go out and fight and die for you and never know the difference. And you tryin' to use me and my dead boy's memory to make out like everybody's all satisfied here in the land of the free, that we's all "one big happy family" who's just tickled to death with the

American Way!

Well, I don't know nothin' 'bout no other kinda way. I ain't never been on no trips to Europe or Russia or China or any of them places that I hears the man talk about on the radio, and I don't know what they does anywhere else. But I do know a whole lot 'bout right here from my whole life of experience. And I say I don't like everything the way it is! And it's high time—way past time—that a lot more changes were made! So that folks like my boy and your boy will have the same chance as anybody else to grow up and enjoy life and live like decent folk without no holdbacks 'cause they're colored.

Yes, Willie's dead and gone now, and I'm proud he was brave and helped save somebody else 'fore he got killed. But I can't help thinkin' Willie died fightin' in the wrong place. [*Quietly intense.*] Willie shoulda had that machine gun over here!

So you can take this medal back on up to Washington and tell them I don't want it! Take it back. Pin it on your own shirt! Give it to the ones who keeps this big lie goin' and send boys like my Willie all over the world to die for some kinda freedom and democracy they always gets the leavin's of! You done a pretty good job. You had folks fooled a long time with all this honey-talk, an' you even had me readin' off your words for you. But I done woke up! I knows what you're tryin' to do and I ain't gonna let you do it to me no more! Here! Take it back! [*She hurls the medal at the General. He ducks in terror...*]

★

Scene from
BACCALAUREATE
by William Branch

CHARACTERS:
ANGELA WILLIAMS: Attractive graduate student at the university.
DOCKERY HILL: A self-described "working man" in his late thirties.
MARTHA HILL: Doc's wife, Angela's older sister.

SETTING: The entire action of the play occurs in the apartment of the Hills, an African-American family, on the second floor of a two-family house in a mid-Western university town during a spring in the late 1950's.

[There is silence for a moment. Then quick footsteps are heard on the steps outside. The door opens to admit ANGELA WILLIAMS. *She is a quite attractive young woman in her early twenties, and she carries an armful of textbooks. She closes the door and leans against it, blowing at the exertion of running up the stairs.]*

ANGELA: *[Looks around.]* Martha? *[Goes into the bedroom and looks in.]* Martha, anybody home? *[Satisfied she puts her books down on the sofa, takes off her light jacket and starts for the bathroom. Just then the flush of the commode is heard, and an instant later DOC emerges, wiping his neck with a towel flung over his shoulder. He stops upon seeing ANGELA].* Oh. Hi, Doc.

DOC: Hi.

ANGELA: Is Martha Home?

DOC: Yeah, she's...*[Glances around.]* out in back of someplace.

ANGELA: Why, Doc, that's my towel!

DOC: *[Looks at it.]* Is it? Oh, I hadn't noticed. Guess I just grabbed up the first thing handy.

ANGELA: *[Taking it from him.]* I wish you'd stick to your own towels. I have enough laundry of my own to take care of now, without having to wash behind you, too. [*Makes a move as if to go past him. He stands with arms folded and smiles. She feints to his other side, but he does not budge.*] Doc, I have to go to the bathroom. [**ANGELA** *hesitates, then tries to move past him quickly. He reaches out and grabs her.*]

ANGELA: Doc! Doc! Stop it. You let me go!

DOC: [*Pulling her to him.*] I'm not gonna hurt you, Angela, I just want you to be nice to me.

ANGELA: [*Struggling.*] Will you stop it, Doc! If you don't, I'm going to tell Martha on you!

DOC: [*Trying to kiss her.*] You wouldn't wanna do that! Now would you—

ANGELA: Doc! Do you hear me? Doc—stop it! [*Manages to break his hold and runs away a few steps.*]

DOC: [*Breathes heavily and grins.*] Hell, you can't blame a guy for tryin', can you? [*He takes a step toward her. She darts quickly into the bathroom and slams the door. Just then* **MARTHA** *is seen climbing the back stairs.* **DOC** *glances up quickly and strides into the bedroom, where he busies himself putting on his shirt.* **MARTHA** *enters the kitchen and continues through to the bedroom.*]

MARTHA: Doc, you're just going to have to do something about that Dickie. He's getting out of hand.

DOC: What'd he do now?

MARTHA: He's been out there fighting over Charlie's bike...

DOC: Well, I told you to get him one of his own.

MARTHA: But I don't want Dickie to have a bicycle. You just don't know, I have trouble enough now keeping the kids near home, God only knows where they'd be or what they'd be doing if they had a bike to go running around on.

DOC: [*Rolling up his sleeves.*] Aw, you're bringin' 'em up to be a bunch a' faggots, that's what.

MARTHA: Well, if you were home more often, maybe you could do better!

DOC: Hell, how can I be home when I'm workin' three jobs to take care of this crew! And then, when I do get home, what do I have to put up with? A wife who won't sleep with her husband!

MARTHA: You brought it all on yourself.

DOC: The hell I did! [*The commode is heard to flush.*]

MARTHA: [*Looks up.*] Who's that?

DOC: Your sister, who'd you think?

MARTHA: Oh. She had a call a while ago from that Roger Sampson.

DOC: [*Combing his hair.*] Yeah? What'd he want?

MARTHA: I don't know. Said he'd call back later, wouldn't leave a message. First time he's called here in a long time.

DOC: Never would be soon enough.

MARTHA: Now, what have you got against Roger Sampson? He never did anything to you. He's a nice boy from a nice family, and he got his law degree last winter.

DOC: Huh! Who the hell cares about him gettin' a law degree? Law degree, bachelor's degree, master's degree— that's all I ever hear around here! Well, just you let me tell you one thing: I'd rather' be just what I am, see? A custodian. Custodian—that's French for just plain ordinary hardworkin' janitor, and that's what I am. I'd rather be just that, see? A janitor with three buildings to take care of, than one a' them punk-ass smart-aleck niggers with a "coilitch" degree, walkin' around dressed so sharp all the time, ain't got one nickel to rub against the other!

MARTHA: Well, Doc, nobody said anything about you.

DOC: [*Wound up.*] And another thing! I don't see you complainin' when time comes to pay the bills around here about the kind of work I do! I'm workin' three buildings, three different jobs, to make enough money to takes care of you and the kids. Yeah, and that smart-ass sister of yours, too!

MARTHA: Shh, Doc! She'll hear you. Besides, you know Angela's in school. She does the best she can, she pays her board.

DOC: Hah! The money she puts into this house wouldn't take care of the ship paper for a week. And I don't care if she does hear me!

MARTHA: Doc!

DOC: And the way she walks around with that superior air of hers. "Hi, Doc" and "Good-bye, Doc" that's all she ever says to me!

MARTHA: [*Suspicion forming.*] Doc...Doc, ha've you been after Angela again?

DOC: What? Are you kiddin'? What for?

MARTHA: You know what for! Doc, you know I warned you the last time.

DOC: Well for chris'sakes—this is ridiculous! Who said I been after her, did she say anything to you? Huh?

MARTHA: No. But—

DOC: Well, what're you talkin' about, then? Shee-it, here I am workin' my ass off and she accuses me of a thing like that. [*From a distance, the clock tower begins tolling the hour, after which it strikes five.* DOC *speaks at the first chime.*] There gimme my hat! I gotta go to work. [*Picks up his hat and jams it onto his head.*]
MARTHA: [*Following him to the door.*] Don't you want something to eat?

DOC: Naw, I'm not hungry. Just have my dinner hot for me when I get back at nine. [*Goes out, slamming the door. Just then* **ANGELA** *emerges from the bathroom and starts for her room.*]

ANGELA: Oh—hi, Martha.

MARTHA: [*Gazing at* **ANGELA** *reflectively.*] Hi...

ANGELA: [*Stops.*] Whoa! What's the matter?

MARTHA: Matter? Oh, nothing. Nothing at all.

ANGELA: Well, you certainly have got a peculiar look on your face.

MARTHA: Have I? I didn't mean to. [*There is a pause.* **ANGELA** *starts to gather up her books.*]

MARTHA: Uh, Angela.

ANGELA: Yes?

MARTHA: Has, uh...has Doc said anything to you lately?

ANGELA: Said anything? Like what?

MARTHA: You know. Like before.

ANGELA: Oh, Martha, you know better than that. Whatever put such a silly question in your head?

MARTHA: Then he hasn't, huh?

ANGELA: Of course not! Honestly, Martha, sometimes I don't know what to think about you.

MARTHA: [*A little sheepish.*] Well, I didn't know. You know, Doc and I haven't been getting along so well lately.

ANGELA: I know. [*Smiles.*] Dickie told me you slept in his bed last night.

MARTHA: [*Blushes.*] Yeah...I—I guess it seems kind of silly. But, then, you don't know what Doc said about me.

ANGELA: Oh, yes I do. Gracie told me all about it.

MARTHA: [*Sits disgustedly.*] Gracie! Honestly, Angela, I just don't understand Gracie anymore! Why did she have to go and discuss this with everybody in town before she even told me, her own sister?

ANGELA: Well, you know her better than I do. You two came along together.

MARTHA: And I'll bet she's even written down home to Momma about it by now.

ANGELA: Now Martha, Gracie wouldn't do a thing like that.

MARTHA: Oh, yes she would, too, you just don't know.

ANGELA: Well, anyway, you aren't going to have a baby now, are you? So forget about it.

MARTHA: Forget about it? How can I forget about a thing like that! And the thing that hurts most is I really wanted to have another baby.

ANGELA: You did!

MARTHA: Yes, I was so happy when I thought I was pregnant. It was such a lovely feeling, thinking that again I was going to be able to bring another life into the world. Another brand-new person that would never have even been, if it hadn't been for me. Well, me and Doc. I—I guess I sound rather silly, Angela, but that's the way I felt. For a whole two weeks I went around the house just singing, I was so happy. And...and then...After I told Doc, and he didn't sound so happy about it...And after the doctor told me it was a mistake. And then to hear from Grace about the awful things that Doc said, oh, I was crushed! Just crushed, that's all. You don't know how it feels, Angela. You've never had a baby to cuddle in your arms and hold at your breast. And you've never had a husband who could hurt you so.

ANGELA: Thank God!

MARTHA: Oh! By the way, I meant to tell you. Roger Sampson called.

ANGELA: He did? When?

MARTHA: About half an hour ago. I asked him if there was any message, but he said he'd call you back later.

ANGELA: [*Reflectively.*] I see. Thanks,

MARTHA: [*Clears her throat.*] Roger hasn't called in quite some time now, has he?

ANGELA: All right, Martha. You don't have to pry.

MARTHA: Well, I'm not prying, I'm just interested. After all, I did promise Momma I'd take care of you.

ANGELA: [*Rises and takes up her books again.*] Well, you don't have to bother. I'm a big girl now, twenty-three, remember? And I'm perfectly capable of taking care of my own affairs. [*Goes into her room.*]

MARTHA: I'm sure you can, Angela, but I just thought it might be rather nice if you wanted to...to discuss them with someone a little older and more experienced than yourself.

ANGELA: [*From her room.*] No, thank you! It's precisely that: discussing your affairs with your older sister that's got you into all your trouble now!

MARTHA: [*Hurt.*] Well, if that's the way you feel, you can take your own phone calls from now on!

★

monologue and scene from
THE FABULOUS MISS MARIE
by Ed Bullins

Ed Bullins has written numerous plays, among them, many award winners. He has also written fiction, poetry and criticism. Currently, he writes, studies, acts, directs and produces in the San Francisco Bay Area.

Mr. Bullins is Producing Playwright of The BMT Theatre of Emeryville, California. He teaches African American Humanities and Theatre (literature, history and critical ideology) at Contra Costa College in San Pablo, California. He recently co-wrote with Idris Ackamoor the musical drama, *I Think It's Gonna Turn Out Fine*, which was done last year at Manhattan's La Mama E.T.C. and in Japan, and is being done in Vienna, Austria this year. Bullins also wrote with Ackamoor, the autobiographical play, *American Griot*, which premiered at La Mama last winter.

Ed Bullins' one-act *Salaam, Huey Newton, Salaam* was part of the Ensemble Studio Theatre Festival of New One Act Plays and is included in Best Short Plays of 1990.

Mr. Bullins has written many plays, many of them produced throughout the United States and abroad. Among his better-known work is *The Taking of Miss Janie* ("Best American Play" 1974/75 New York Drama Critics), *The Duplex*, *The Electronic Nigger* (Obie, Drama Desk Award) and *A Son, Come Home* (Obie Award). He is the author of collections of his own plays, a novel and a book of short prose—*The Hungered One*, *The Duplex*, *Four Dynamite Plays*, *The Theme Is Blackness* (all Morrow), *The Reluctant Rapist* (Harper & Row) and *Five Plays by Ed Bullins* (Bobbs-Merrill). He has edited two anthologies of plays, *New Plays From the Black Theatre* (Bantam) and *The New Lafayette Theatre Presents* (Doubleday/Anchor).

SCENE: The music plays and the lights and TV's glare throws strange patterns across the stage.

MARIE: What chou say?...I been drinkin' Scotch for quite some time now...ever since I got accustomed to tryin' to live like I would like to become accustomed to...ha ha...damn right I do. I used to live in Buffalo, ya know I'm really from Pittsburgh...you understand, but I used to live in Buffalo with my granny...just like Wanda lives here with me...but god knows I wasn't stupid like

Wandie...god knows I wasn't. Damn I was a slick little chick. That's when I started bein' called Miss Marie...It used to snow real deep up in Buffalo and I had my little red boots that I used to tip 'round in...and everybody used to say: "There goes little cute Miss Marie down...to get a bucket of beer for her Granny." And that's where I'd be on my way to...and I'd get there and get inside where it was warm by the coal stove and blow my breath into my hands and take my bucket around to the back end of the bar...that's where they filled your bucket back 'round the side there back in those days. And it ain't had nothin' to do with discrimination...I'm from the North...and I ain't never known anything 'bout no discrimination...I always did have my freedom...Yes sir, Miss Marie will tell you...I want to thank you. [*The Christmas tree glows and pulsates dimly to the rhythm of the scene, as the television casts its mute image outward, and the phonograph plays softly.*] If I couldn't have my Scotch every day, honey...I'd quit! I'd just give it up, baby. Naw...I ain't kiddin'...Hummp. And it better be Ambassador too. Those old cows in my clubs would swear that I was slippin' if they saw me sippin' a Miller's High Life...Wouldn't they?...Yeah...sure would. Bad as me havin' no fur coat. Marie Horton...without even a stole. Ohhh...that Bill...he says I don't need a fur in Los Angeles. Sheet...I've had a fur ever since my granny gave me my first one when I was nine...'cept now that we out here...You know I'm president of three Negro women's clubs...really the founder as well as president. And I have to keep myself together...or what would the girls say? Hell, I know what they'd say...They'd say: "Who does Miss Marie"...that's what they call me,"Miss Marie"..."Who does Miss Marie think she is?"...they'd say..."she hasn't even got a fur coat." they'd say..."Every time you see her she's in that old red print dress with her fat gut stickin' out so far it looks like the middle button's gonna pop off" they would say. "Probably needs to wear her house dress, poor dear, with that little bit of money Bill brings in" they would say...if I stood for them 'n let them...Shoot...I ain't never gonna let them say nothin' about Marie Horton. Naw suh! That's for somebody else to tolerate...not Miss Marie...We been out here in L.A. for twelve years now, Bill and me. Came out a couple years after the war. And it's groovy, baby...nothin' but high life. Bill makes three times as much...maybe four...as he made back East. He used to dance before he went out and had to get a job. Yeah. I don't know how anybody can stay back there in the cold. Give me L.A. any day, baby. It's got everything...And the men...the men...makes a girl like me drool all over her cocktail frock...'cause this is the place to keep an old hen scratchin' like a spring bird. Ooooo...yeah. In the warm California sun. [*She does a large bump and grind, snaps her fingers and humps the audience. Grinds grimacing as if during orgasm.*] You can take it if you can make it 'cause you ain't gonna break it, yeah. Miss Marie wants to thank you....Bill brings home two hundred stone cold dollars a week...to me, Miss Marie...and puts it in my hand. And the tips he makes parkin' cars out to the studio in Beverly Hills is more than that. We make almost as much as some colored doctors make...'n we spend it too. Cause it's party time every day at Miss Marie's house...[**MARIE** *and* **BILL** *are seen.*]

MARIE: Did you have to take her around our friends, Bill? Did you have to take that white woman where we go?

BILL: I was drunk, Marie...High as a kite...It shouldn't have happened, I know, but I just couldn't help it.

MARIE: [*Resigned.*] No...I guess you couldn't...You done so much to me over the years...I guess doin' just one more thing like this don't really matter.

BILL: But, baby, if we could...if we could...

MARIE: Well, I can't...you saw to that, didn't you?

BILL: ...If we could have only had kids, Marie.

MARIE: It was the abortion that did it. It was that damn quack that you got me that messed me up for life.

BILL: I never wanted you to do it, Marie.

MARIE: It was your fault, Bill Horton! It was your fault! You got me pregnant!

BILL: But I never wanted you to get that operation. I never wanted you to get rid of the baby.

MARIE: But the other one went okay...Nothing happened to me after the first one.

BILL: Your grandmother saw to that.

MARIE: Granny had her place in the community....Granny couldn't have me do something terrible like that and ruin our good family name.

BILL: But you should have never gotten rid of our baby, Marie.

MARIE: But I could have never had a baby by that ole nigger from The Hill....I couldn't do that to Granny, Bill...

BILL: It would have been so nice if...

MARIE: If you just hadn't told our friends...I would have let you keep her quietly...as long as you kept up my house.

BILL: I was drunk...drunk as a skunk...and I wanted the world to know that I could have kids even if she was white.

MARIE: You shouldn't have gotten me pregnant....You shouldn't have been younger than me and got me pregnant...and give in to me and gotten the operation for me like Granny had...and married me 'cause you ruined me...That's right, Bill, we wouldn't have been married now...and out of love.

BILL: Sometimes when I get drunk I'm sorry afterwards... sometimes...[*Lights and shapes alter; the Christmas tree glows from the darkness. The dog yaps outside.*]

★

monologue from
BESSIE SMITH SPEAKS
by China Clark

_____

BESSIE: Smooth tongued Negro, in a night light.
Tall and Dark
Young and Firm
The man gave my heart a terrible turn.
He smelled like lilac
On a spring day
He smelled like fresh cut grass
After a moonlight roll in the hay.
Those first moments
Those first hours
Flowers!

Nobody knows the sweetness two lovers share in the Silence. The first moments of love. I don't think it will last forever. But it changes your life forever. For a moment I had something else to live for, beside show business and my family. From the moment I laid my eyes on Jack I could see no one else, not in a real way. I had my moment, my affairs on the road! Jack could never understand a woman takin' care of her needs. He was old fashioned that way. [*To audience.*] You in the back? [*Pauses to hear the question.*] What made me choose Jack? He was my KNIGHT IN SHINING ARMOR and I trusted him. I trusted him from the start, I knew I was his only STAR! I could see it in his eyes. [*To audience.*] You back there in the far right corner—What you say? [*Pauses.*] Now that's a good question, especially for a blues singer. "What makes a woman love a man like I loved my Husband Jack Gee?" It was the way he made me feel. When I was with him everything was right in the world.

★

scene from
NEFFIE'S DANCE
by China Clark

SCENE: NEFFIE's room is stage right, down right. The bed sits parallel to the audience, in back of the bed is a suspended window. The set is surrealistic. To the left of the bed is a small night table, a black flower is laying on it. Propped up beside the head of the bed is AMIRI's rifle. Also suspended at a right angle in front of the bed, is NEFFIE's dreaming glassless mirror; it is long enough for her to walk through. As the lights come up slowly, NEFFIE is dancing in front of her mirror, very slight sounds are heard of the busy African Village of her dream.

TIME: July 13, 1967, midnight, it is the night of the Newark New Jersey riot.

[*We hear the gentle beat of the Afro drum, underneath is the sound of the violence in the streets. Amiri is laying on* **NEFFIE'***s bed, her room is dimly lit. Amiri is wearing a gray uniform jacket.* **NEFFIE** *is doing a slow sensuous dance for him, moving to the Afro beat in front of her mirror.*]

NEFFIE: [*Finishing her dance, going over to him.*] I love you Amiri, smile for me.

AMIRI: [*A faint smile.*] I know, but you'd better be quiet I don't want you to wake your mother up. If she finds me in here, we'll be having a funeral tomorrow instead of a wedding.

NEFFIE: I think it's so romantic.

AMIRI: [*Listening to the gun fire.*] What?

NEFFIE: You coming here to see me, on a night like this.

AMIRI: I couldn't stand going through this night without you close to me. Tonight, the old world is burning, tomorrow, we'll start to build a new one, right here, the revolution has only just begun.

NEFFIE: And so have we. I'll be right by your side, I'd be happy with you no matter what your job was—a slave, a street cleaner, a revolutionary—It doesn't matter to me, as long as you love me.

AMIRI: Everybody loves you but after tomorrow, you'll be all mine.

NEFFIE: I'm all yours now.

AMIRI: [*Jokingly.*] Just a few more hours and, good-bye mama Henderson. [*Amiri looks through the window again.*] There's a war going on outside, and I feel like I'm the cause of it.

NEFFIE: You didn't make the world, you're only trying to improve it. Here feel this.

AMIRI: [*Playfully.*] No. If I feel that, I'll never go.

NEFFIE: Oh, come on, feel my heart, put your ear to it, listen closely it sounds like the drums of Africa, a primitive far away place where our souls are at rest. There is no war going on in there. It's peaceful...Sometimes it beats so loud, the sound comes from outside of my body...it draws me into my mirror. I'm transformed, standing naked in the sun, with flamingos flying above my head. I hear the sound of water running down the side of a mountain, so I run towards the sound, then I see you standing there King of the mountain, you're naked too, then I sit at the bottom and open my legs to you, as wide as I can, so you can get a good view. Then you come running and take me in your arms and we whirl and whirl until we turn into pure light.

AMIRI: I feel guilty.

NEFFIE: Why?

AMIRI: Hold me.

NEFFIE: What is it?

AMIRI: Two children were shot today.

NEFFIE: I heard.

AMIRI: I feel so responsible, the police said one of the kids was stealing a case of beer, while his friend covered him with a pointed gun. They shot both of them one in the back, when my men got there they said the boy had a water gun—he thought it was a game, a kid's game. "We hold these truths to be self evident, that all men are created equal" I'm fighting for that idea, not against it.

NEFFIE: If you had taken a gun to those children's heads yourself you wouldn't have killed them. You can't kill life or Soul or Spirit. It's all a dream and when the world wakes up they will realize that only Love is left.

AMIRI: For once, Neffie, just for once, can you come down out of that place where you hide and talk to me.

NEFFIE: You said we needed a crisis to progress with well this is our ultimate-demonstration. The people are mad as hell and armed in the streets, no one can be hurt because the cause is just, the motives are right. You took a stand and the people love you for it. You gave them a sword, the spirit of freedom is a sweet thing Amiri, and you gave it to them.

AMIRI: I'm sorry, all I want now is the silence of the guns, the light of the morning, and you.

[MRS. HENDERSON: [Calling from off stage.] Neffie? Neffie? [AMIRI rises, starts to leave by the window, NEFFIE stops him.]

NEFFIE: Yes mama?

[MRS. HENDERSON: Is something wrong? I thought I heard voices? Do you want me to come and sleep with you?]

NEFFIE: [Smiling to AMIRI.] No mama, I'm fine.
[MRS. HENDERSON: Get to sleep then. We've got to get up early in the morning.]

NEFFIE: Yes, Mama.

[MRS. HENDERSON: Oh, Neffie, sleep on your stomach, so you won't have those dreams again.]

NEFFIE Yes, Mama, goodnight Mama.

AMIRI: I'd better go now.

NEFFIE: No, wait until daybreak. It's too dangerous for you out there. If something would happened to you, I would burn for the rest of my life. No one to put out my fire.

AMIRI: If I ever catch anyone coming near your fire, I'll kill him.

NEFFIE: It's been a long time for us. I can remember loving you from my mother's womb. I was curled up in there all quiet and warm, longing for the day that I would be born again to be in your arms.

AMIRI: Here before I forget. It's a wedding present.

NEFFIE: A silver bracelet.

AMIRI: It's from Africa, it belonged to a necromancer.

NEFFIE: I'll wear it always, I have a gift for you, I've written it down. [*Reading the poem to him.*]
There are poems that tell of sadness
There are poems that tell of joy
But this poem of love I write to you
Has never been told before
For I can't remember one night when I did not love you
I don't know where you came from
I don't know where you've been
But I've loved you my whole life through
And now that you are so close to me
I love you so much
I don't know what to do
Before I found you, I loved you, and after you've gone
My love will live on and on and on
For I can't remember one moment when I did not love you
My love is like the sea
A never ending cycle
I have longed throughout eternity to feel your
Warm body next to mine.
My spirit has not rested since the beginning of time
For, I can't remember one moment that I did not love you.

AMIRI: Beautiful, what gets into you, to make you glow like that?

NEFFIE: Love, Love gets into me. Remember that first night we spent together under the mountain?

AMIRI: Yes, sometimes that's all I can remember, and when I do I'm free, free for the demonstrations, the marches, the protests.

NEFFIE: [*Laying beside him.*] You're free because you know love. You're a shepherd under orders from the divine mind of Love.

AMIRI: [*Bombs are heard in the background.*] Poems, Love making, I wish we could always be there in our place, under that tree, and have this whole crazy damn world under there with us, I wish I could take them all, turn them into my manhood, and shove them into you as far as I can get then they would all stop hating each other, they would all work together, dedicating their lives to trying to get back into you.

NEFFIE: There's a tree behind the mountain
Growing tall against the night
There's a tree behind the mountain
Where her love and her did light.

AMIRI: Another wedding present?

NEFFIE: No, just a thought. Lets get away from Mama and the others soon, right after the wedding.

AMIRI: O. K. Baby. [*They lay in each others arms,* **NEFFIE** *goes to sleep,* **AMIRI** *quietly takes his gun and leaves by the window but, before he goes, he says:*] I love you.

★

scene from
MEDAL OF HONOR RAG
by Tom Cole

Tom Cole's *Medal of Honor Rag* first appeared in New York at the Theatre de Lys in 1976; Woodie King, Jr., was among the producers and Howard Rollins played the lead. After many productions nationwide and overseas, it was televised in the first season of PBS's American Playhouse in 1982, starring Hector Elizondo and Damien Leake, directed by Lloyd Richards. Tom Cole's other plays include *Fighting Bod*, *Dead Souls* (from Gogol), and *About Time*.

He has written award-winning fiction, translated from Russian and Italian, made documentary films and written features, including Smooth Talk, with Laura Dern and Treat Williams (directed by Joyce Chopra), which won Grand Prize at the U.S. Film Festival and was one of the New York Times' "ten best" films of 1986.

D.J.: [*Laughs.*] Oh, man...Oh, my...Suppose I didn't have that medal...You wouldn't be here, right? You wouldn't know me from a hole in the wall. I mean, I would be invisible to you. Like a hundred thousand other dudes that got themselves sent over there to be shot at by a lot of little Chinamen hiding up in the trees. I mean, you're some famous Doctor, right? Because, you know, I'm a special case! Well I am, I am one big tidbit. I am what you call a "hot property" in this man's Army. Yes, sir! I am an authentic hero, a showpiece. One look at me, enlistments go up 200%...I am a credit to my race. Did you know that? I am an honor to the city of Detroit, to say nothing of the state of Michigan, of which I am the only living Medal of Honor winner! I am a feather in the cap of the Army, a flower in the lapel of the military—I mean, I am quoting to you, man! That is what they say at banquets, given in my honor! Yes, sir! And look at me! Look at me! [*Pointing to himself in the clothing of a sick man, in an office of an Army hospital.*]

DOCTOR: There was a truck.

D.J.: A truck?

DOCTOR: First day in Vietnam. F.N.G. You hitched a ride in a truck.

D.J.: Jesus.

DOCTOR: Don't feel like talking about it?

D.J.: No, I don't.

DOCTOR: That's as good a reason as any for telling me.

D.J.: [*Reacts to this notion, but then goes along with it. Sits down again, as he gets into the story.*] Well, uh...we were riding along, in the truck. Real hot, you know, and nobody much was around...and we see there's a bunch of kids, maybe three, four of them crossing the road up ahead...You know?

DOCTOR: How old were they?

D.J.: Well, it's hard to tell. Those people are all so small, you know?—I mean, all dried-up and tiny, man...maybe ten years old, twelve, I don't know...

DOCTOR: And?

D.J.: Well, we see they're being pretty slow getting out of the road, so we got to swerve a little bit to miss them...Not a lot, you know, but a little bit. This seems to make the guys in the back of the truck really mad. Like, somebody goes, "Little fuckers!" You know?...Then those kids, as soon as we pass, they start laughing at us, and give us the finger. Know what I mean? [**D.J.** *gives the* **DOCTOR** *the finger, to illustrate. The* **DOCTOR** *starts to laugh, but then puts his hand to his head, as if knowing what is to come.*] Yeah. So I'm thinking to myself, "Now where did they learn to do that? That ain't some old oriental custom. They musta learned it from our guys.''...Suddenly the guys on the truck start screaming for the driver to back up. So he jams on the brakes, and in this big cloud of dust he's grinding this thing in reverse as if he means to run those kids down, backwards. The kids start running away, of course, but one of 'em, maybe two, I don't know, they stop, you see, and give us the finger again, from the side of the road. And they're laughing...So, uh,...everybody on the truck opens fire. I mean, I couldn't believe it, they're pouring all this firepower into these kids. The kids are lying on the ground, they're dead about a hundred times over, and these guys are still firing rounds into their bodies, like they've gone crazy. And the kids' bodies are giving these little jumps into the air like rag dolls, and then they flop down again...

DOCTOR: [*Very quiet.*] What happened then?

D.J.: They just sorta stopped, and me and these guys drove away. [**DOCTOR** *waits.*] I'm thinking to myself, you know, what is going on here? I must be out of tune. My first day in the country, and we ain't even reached the Combat Zone! I'm thinking, like, this is the enemy? Kids who make our trucks give a little jog in the road and give us the finger? I mean, come on, man!...And one guy, he sees I'm sort of staring back down the road, so he gives me like this, you know—[**D.J.** *simulates a jab of the elbow.*] and he says, "See how we hose them li'l motherfuckers down, man? Hose 'em down. You like that?...And they're all blowing smoke away from their muzzles and checking their weapons down, like they're a bunch of gunslingers, out of the Old West...[**D.J.** *shaking his head. He still has trouble believing he saw this.*]

DOCTOR: [*Measured.*] Why do you think they did all that?

D.J.: I don't know. They went crazy, that's why?

DOCTOR: Went crazy...Were all those soldiers White?

D.J.: I don't remember

DOCTOR: What do you think?

D.J.: [*A little dangerously.*] I think some of them were White. [*Waits.* **D.J.** *does not add anything.*]

DOCTOR: And what did you do?

D.J.: What do you mean, what did I do?

DOCTOR: Well, did you report them to a superior officer?

D.J.: [*Explodes.*] Superior Officer? What superior officer? Their fucking lieutenant was right there in the fucking truck, he was the first one to open fire! I mean what are you talking about, man? Don't you know what is going on over there?

DOCTOR: Why get mad at me? I didn't shoot those children.

D.J.: [*Confused, angry.*] God damn...! [*Glaring at the* **DOCTOR.**] I mean, what are you accusing me of, man?

DOCTOR: I'm not accusing you of anything.

D.J.: Well, I'm asking you! What would you have done? You think you're so much smarter and better than me? You weren't there, man! That's why you can sit here and be the judge! Right? [*No reaction from the* **DOCTOR,** *except for a tic of nervousness under the extreme tension that has been created.*] I mean, look at you sitting there in your suit, with that shit-eating grin on your face!

DOCTOR: You're getting mad at my suit again? You think my suit has caused these problems? [**DALE JACKSON** *can't control his rage and frustration any longer. He blows up, grabs his chair as the only object available—and swings it above his head as a weapon. The* **DOCTOR** *instinctively ducks away and shouts at him to stop; shouting—improvised.*] Wait a minute! Sergeant! Stop it! [**D.J.** *crashes the chair against the desk, or the floor. He cannot vent his physical aggression directly against the* **DOCTOR.** *After he has torn up the room,* **D.J.** *stands, exhausted, confused, empty-handed. While* **D.J.** *subsides.*] Are you all right? [**D.J.** *stares at the* **DOCTOR,** *panting. He moves away into the silence of the room.* **DOCTOR** *neutrally.*] How did you feel about being a killer?

D.J.: I didn't kill those kids, man!

DOCTOR: I didn't say you did! Did I? [*Waits,* **D.J.** *glares at him, still full of rage and suspicion. But a deep point has been made, and both men are aware of it. After a pause.*] Did you ever tell people at home about any of this? About Dakto, about the truck?

D.J.: No. I didn't.

DOCTOR: Didn't they ask? Didn't anyone ever wonder why you came home early?

D.J.: Yeah, they asked.

DOCTOR: Who asked?

D.J.: My mother. Little kids, sometimes. My girl, Bea...

DOCTOR: Sounds like everybody.

D.J.: No, not everybody. A lot of people didn't give a shit about what happened.

DOCTOR: And you pretended you didn't give a shit, either?

D.J.: What do you want me to say, man?

DOCTOR: But what did you say when your mother or your friends asked you?

D.J.: You guess. You're the specialist.

DOCTOR: [*After a pause.*] All right, I will. You said, "Nothing happened. Nothing happened over there."

D.J.: Right on. Word for word.

DOCTOR: It's in the folder.

D.J.: Yeah, sure.

DOCTOR: [*Takes words from report in the folder.*] It also says you "lay up in your room a lot, staring at the ceiling..." [*The* **DOCTOR** *waits, to see if* **D.J.** *has anything to add.*]

D.J.: Read. Read, man. I'm tired.

DOCTOR: Did you do that—did that happened to you right away?

D.J.: Right away...? No. Well, at first I felt pretty good, considering... [*Trails off.*] Considering, uh...

DOCTOR: Considering that you had just been heavily narcotized, tied up in a straitjacket, and shipped home in a semi-coma. After surviving a hell of death and horror, which by all odds should have left you dead yourself.

D.J.: Yeah. Considering that.

DOCTOR: You felt lucky that you had survived? At first?

D.J.: I just used to like going to bars with my cousin, William...my friends. I was glad to see my girl, Beatrice, and my mama. I joked around with them. I tried to be good to them...I shot baskets with the kids, down the block. Understand?

DOCTOR: Of course. And then what happened?

D.J.: It didn't last.

DOCTOR: And?

D.J.: I started laying up in my room. Staring at the ceiling.

DOCTOR: But what happened? What changed you?

D.J.: I don't remember.

DOCTOR: But you did go numb?

D.J.: You're talking me around in circles, Doctor!

DOCTOR: I'm sorry. This terrible delayed reaction, after a kind of relief—it seems so mysterious, but it's the common pattern for men who went through your kind of combat trauma...

D.J.: [*With irony.*] Well, I'm glad to hear that. But I sometimes began to suspect that my girl, Bea, might just prefer a man what can see and hear and think and feel things. And do things! You follow my meaning? A man what can walk and talk and stuff like that?

DOCTOR: Did you stop having sexual relations with her?

D.J.: Well, I have been trying to send you signals, man! You're none too quick on the pick-up.

DOCTOR: Did she criticize you?

D.J.: Not about that...She wanted me to get a job, so we could get married.

DOCTOR: Well. The job situation must have been difficult in Detroit.

D.J.: Especially if you lay up in your room all day, staring at the ceiling. Funny thing about the city of Detroit—not too many people come up through your bedroom offering you a job, on most days. Did you know that?

DOCTOR: I've heard that, yes...Did you stop getting out of bed altogether?

D.J.: No, I put my feet to the floor once in a while. Used to go on down to the V.A. and stand in line for my check.

DOCTOR: How did they treat you down there, at the Veteran's

Office?

D.J.: Like shit.

★

scene from
HOMEGIRLS
by Karen Evans

Homegirls is about five young women and SNCC, the Student Non-Violent Coordinating Committee which was the student organization, in the vanguard of the civil rights movement. SNCC has been struggling with which type of action to take, nonviolent protest and voter registration or the more aggressive freedom rides. They have decided they can do both, but it means breaking up, sending some people to different places which will be new to them since they launched the Fisk Student Sit-Ins together as one group.

The five women, TK, Mary, Reba, Jenny, and Barbara are very close friends who have grown even closer because of the movement. They are vehemently opposed to having SNCC break up to take different paths, feeling that they don't want to be separated and simply can't continue without the support they have given each other. They are all worried about Reba's relationship with Dexter, because he is so smooth and seems to manipulate her to his advantage politically.

SCENE: A field at the stadium. A row of bleachers is center stage. REBA and MARY slowly jog by in gray sweat suits. They jog offstage. They jog back on stage.

TIME: December 1959.

REBA: You know, if I'd known physical education was part of freshman year, I'd a though twice about staying home and helping Aunt Mamie with the store. It's cold out here. God, that's Willie T. Osbourne!

MARY: Who's that?

REBA: He personally terrorized every high school football team in Doughtery County.

MARY: Do you know him?

REBA: Not personally—not yet, anyway. He was there last week Barbara was hit. [**MARY** *and* **REBA**'s *eyes follow the imaginary* *class as they pass by them.*]

REBA: [*Eyeing* **WILLIE.**] There's Willie again. Sweating is so unladylike! Do I look alright from behind in this tight thing?

MARY: We've hardly done enough to work up a sweat, Reba. It's not that bad.

REBA: Running around a track *four* times? And plus with the humiliation of being passed—twice?

MARY: Don't complain, I'm keeping you company. [*Pointedly.*] I wouldn't leave you in the blink of an eye like some other people I know.

REBA: What are you talking about?

MARY: You all left for dinner without me. That's the third time this week.

REBA: You upset about that? I can't believe it!

MARY: Don't stop, they'll pass us again. Yes, I am upset. Three times in one week?

REBA: It was just an accident, gee whiz, it just happened.

MARY: [*Stops running.*] It wasn't by accident. I got left because I'm the White girl.

REBA: That's not true, we think of you as one of us.

MARY: No, you don't. Like when everybody's running their mouth and Jenny or TK or Barbara says nigger and suddenly you remember I'm there.

REBA: Barbara never says nig...that word.

MARY: Nigger.

REBA: Niggah.

MARY: That's what I said, nigger.

REBA: It's not nig*ger*. When Negroes call each other...that word...they say nig*gah*. When somebody White calls you that they hit the "er" with a nasally kind of twang that's meant to kind of ring in your ears. Besides, we just don't use that word around you cause we know you can't use it.

MARY: I know I can't use it.

REBA: I know you know.

MARY: I know that you know that I know. Why doesn't anybody talk about my being White?

REBA: I don't know. [*Pause.*]

MARY: When I'm not around do you all talk about me?

REBA: ...no...

MARY: [*Disappointed.*] You don't?

REBA: ...Well...

MARY: You mean my name never comes up?

REBA: Yeah, yes it does.

MARY: Good.

REBA: What do you mean good?!

MARY: If nobody talks about me it either means I'm boring or you all don't care about me. What do you all say about me?

REBA: You ask more questions...

MARY: If you tell me what they say about me. I'll tell you what they say about you.

REBA: What you mean, what they say about me?

MARY: Everybody talks about everybody else when that person's not there, but we never talk about what I want to talk about when everybody is there.

REBA: And what in God's name do you want to talk about, Mary?

MARY: About race relations.

REBA: We are all attending the same university in Nashville, Tennessee and it's 1959. We are having race relations.

MARY: Jesus, Reba, what am I suppose to do, go back to California and tell everybody I attended a Negro university for a year and nobody ever said the words Negro and White?

REBA: Renee.

MARY: Reba, Renee, and I don't get it about why you keep calling your Renee. The dorm roster and all the class lists have you as Reba Mazelle Johnson.

REBA: Why, why, why! Mary, you are plucking my last nerve.

MARY: Then just give me some answers and I'll get off the subject. I can't get a handle on all this. Are you my friends or aren't you? I'm three thousand miles from home. Everything seems normal on campus but if I walk downtown with one of you we've got razors up our backs because everybody stares at us. And damn it, all of you, Barbara, Jenny, TK, and you, you get so damn polite to me. And all that good stuff we laughed and talked about in the dorm just isn't there.

REBA: Sure it is. You just let your imagination get the better of you.

MARY: Bullshit.

REBA: [*Angry.*] Mary, did it ever occur to you that Negroes know more about White people than they ever wanted to? And most of what we know we have to know so we can survive? So, Mary, if you want to talk about Whites and Negroes living in harmony, or be part of some great experiment, go do it in Socy 101.

MARY: [**MARY** *sits. Pause.*] You may know about White people, but you don't know a thing about me.

REBA: It would hurt too much to let you in.

MARY: Into what? Where?

REBA: Into my heart.

MARY: I don't understand.

REBA: Being your friend makes me feel raw. There are differences between Negroes and Whites. I learned that as I grew up in the streets and backwoods of Albany.

MARY: Please. I'm not a snake that's going to bite you once you've taken me into your bosom. I'm Mary.

REBA: I'm sorry, I didn't mean to get mad. I don't know how to talk to White people about this.

MARY: Why's it so hard?

REBA: First, nobody White ever asked me to talk about it. Second, it's too ugly to talk about.

MARY: I have to talk about it because I just can't stand being "the White girl."

REBA: I do know what you're talking about.

MARY: I asked you because you're so honest and clear, Reba. Renee. [*They laugh.*]

REBA: We won't ever leave for dinner without you.

MARY: Good. Alright.

REBA: So what do you all say about me when I'm not there?

MARY: [*Teasing.*] Of course, I'm the one that sticks up for you, but TK, TK says...

REBA: Oh my gosh, the rest of the class has gone in, we'll be late, come on, Mary!

[**MARY** *and* **REBA** *exit. Blackout.*]

★

monologue from
MY GIRLISH DAYS
by Karen Evans

Karen is a native of Washington. She attended Eastern High School and was a member of the first class of women at Dartmouth College, where she earned a B.A. in Drama with honors. She returned to Washington and earned an M.F.A. in playwriting from Catholic University. She has won numerous awards in playwriting from the D.C. Commission on the Arts and Humanities and in 1991, won an individual fellowship in playwriting from the National Endowment for the Arts. She has written for the PBS series *WonderWorks* and is writing a feature film script about the only battalion of African American women to serve overseas during World War II. Karen is president and founder of the Black Women Playwrights' Group and is a member of the faculty of the Playwrights' Forum.

This monologue takes place at the climactic scene of the play. In 1939, Gertie, a young Black girl who is very smart and very fast, plots to get out of tiny Hallsboro NC by applying for college without her parents' permission. Her parents discover the plot that she and her best friend Jenny have concocted and stop them. Drawn to Sam Williams, a very popular boy in Hillsboro, she then persuades him to run away to New York with her.

New York is a disaster for them. Sam, a musician, is unable to find work. Gertie finds work. They have a child, LaDonna. The relationship deteriorates and Gertie begins an affair with her boss who is White. Sam finds out and beats her almost to death.

Gertie returns to Hallsboro, broken. She begins working in the shirt factory with her friend Jenny and settles down to a life of drinking too much and sleeping with too many men. Six years later, Sam returns and wants to take LaDonna away from her. She agrees to let her go. In this speech, she gathers her strength and stands up to him.

GERTIE: Were you scared? So was I. Did I let him come to me in a way I coudn't let you come to me? Probably. But you were my missing half. I wanted, expected more from you, and I guess I was just as mad as you were when I didn't get it. You were gonna make me whole. When you start off thinking that something's missing, and the person who's supposed to hand you that missing piece turns to you with hate in their eyes...says, I'm leaving you...

Jenny said goodbye to me tonight. She said she couldn't take it anymore. She was doing new things with her life and they didn't have a thing to do with me. God, that hurt. I asked why can't I do new things, too? Why am I stuck? Frozen? Because I've got unfinished business with you.

There's a moment when you think you're gonna die when you say, this is it, this is my destiny, my fate, what God intended for me. Things are so clear. You stop struggling, fighting for life and just go with it. I went with it and the last thing I remember I was hearing your voice saying, You ain't shit, Gertie.

I thought the fact that I didn't die was wrong. My stupid body didn't listen and give up, too. No! My heart kept pumping because it knew I shouldn't give up and now all of me knows there is a reason to live. I'm going to stop punishing myself. It's time to get on with my life.

When LaDonna came out, you said, There's my girl. I thought she was your girl too, for a long time. I chalked up the fact that she was a good, sweet kid to what she got from you and good luck. As she stood there in that uncomfortable, ruffled concoction, I knew I had given her a whole lot more. She knew who she was. She knew and I helped her learn that.

★

monologue from
SOLOMON'S WAY
by J. e. Franklin

[ANNA: She's almost eighty years old now. What harm can she do to you?]

[EMILE: The least you could-a done, Anna, was to tell me you was planning to do this.]

[ANNA: I didn't mean no harm, dear one...and if you really want me to go in there and tell her to leave, I will. But that would hurt me, 'cause it's like I found me a mother, too.]

EMILE: [*After a beat.*] Why me? Seem like this Solomon thing always happen to me...in some shape, form or fashion. All through my life, even when I was a kid. This little puppy had followed me home, and I kept and fed him for about a month. My mom didn't want me to keep him, but Pop said he didn't have no collar on him so it was finders-keepers-losers-weepers as far as he was concerned. One day, I was playing with him in the yard and here come this man asking questions: "Who gave him to you?" "Where was you at when you found him?" "What day was it?" And such as that. He went up on the porch and knocked on the door and I could feel my heart pounding. He told my Mom and Pop he believed that was his son's puppy. My Mom was gonna make me give him up right then and there, but Pop said "Naw-naw...it don't work like that, sir. You ain't proved this is your son's dog. You bring your son by here to see the dog, and if he recognize and go to him, then we'll see." I'll always love my Pop for that. Next day, they came...him and the boy, 'bout my age, ten or something like that. Sure enough, the dog recognized him, licking all on his face...but he had licked me, too, when he followed me, 'cause he was just friendly like that. I cried and cried and kept a-holt' of him and both of us was just a pulling on him. Pop said that little licking didn't prove the dog was really theirs, and I should have the dog...I was the one been feeding him for thirty days and possession was nine-tenth of the law. "But this dog was born to a litter! You want me to bring the whole litter here and show it to you?" the guy kept-a saying. This kept up for a while and n'ary one of us would yield. Bye-n-bye, a man they called Uncle Titty Baby came up and heard the story. "Take it to Fox! Just take it to Fox!" he kept-a yelling. Who Fox was, see, back then, down there, we didn't go to the courts like we do up here. We had something to settle, we went to the "root-workers" and fortune tellers...not even to the preachers so much. And couldn't nobody settle things like Dr. Fox could! Don't care what you went to him with, he put a period at the end of it, and it stayed there! He could call your friends and your enemies by name without even laying eyes on 'em! And that man could heal, too! Not with needles and all these pills they gives you now'a'days...just them leaves and berries, and some kind-a bones he'd throw like a pair-dice. And him and that snake! [EMILE *chuckles to himself as he remembers fondly.*] Long as three or four train cars! Folks was scared to death of Old Ya-Ya...is what he called the snake. That day, we all showed up...I had the puppy. I had washed and brushed him down. Pop let them tell their story first. Then we told ours, how that boy wasn't even thinking 'bout the puppy til his damn daddy walked by the house and seen me playing with it. Dr. Fox just set there rolling them dry bones. He looked at the other boy, then he looked at me. I could feel myself shaking all over. "Put the dog down," he say. I thought he was telling me to give him to the boy, but he commenced to talking to Old Ya-Ya. We all looked at one another, wondering what he was saying. He stopped talking and listened, like the snake was telling him something. "Ya-Ya want to cut the dog in'to with her tongue and give each boy-half." He said it just as calm. I didn't know a snake couldn't do nothing like that, and I just broke down and cried. That's when the other boy commence to hollering, "Do it...cut him on in'to...lemme see you do it!" Old Fox joog his hand down in a jar and come up with some kind-a powder and pitched it at 'em. Both of 'em jumped up like something had hit 'em...got out-a that shack so fast, I don't even remember seeing 'em leave! I kept that dog till he up and died! [**EMILE** *chuckles to himself, then comes back to the present after a beat.*]

[**ANNA:** I don't think your mother came here to cut you in'to, Emile.]

[EMILE: I don't even know nothing about her.]

[ANNA: You got the chance to find out, Emile. I told her she'd be proud of the man you turned out to be.]

[EMILE: One mind tell me I hate her...another mind say...I don't know what I feel...]

[ANNA: At least she didn't get rid of you before you was born...and she didn't leave you on nobody's doorstep...or in a garbage can, like I was left. And although it hurt me to think my mama left me in such a place to die, still if she was to look for me, I'd gladly throw my arms around her and tell her I forgive her...'cause I know what it is for a young girl to be scared and alone...]

[EMILE: I found out something you don't know, Anna...that she had other children, and she didn't give them away. And that's why I stopped looking for her.]

★

scene from
TWO MENS'ES DAUGHTER
by J. e. Franklin

GOLDIE: Mama wasn't nothing but a kid when she went to work for him. Everywhere she turned, there he was, even after Daddy Randall married her. Ain't many Colored men wants a Colored woman got White men's chill'un, but Daddy Randall loved us just like we was his'n. Old Cecil-Morrow wanted to get even, cheated him out-a some money, mad cause he married Mama. What could a Colored man do back then? He didn't have no rights a White man was bound to respect. I hadn't even quit peeing-the-bed yet the first time I cussed him. I didn't know what I was saying...just repeating words I'd heard the grown-folks use. He told mama to beat me but she wouldn't. That let me know I could keep it up, even after he told me he was my daddy. I told him, "You might-a been the one sired me, but you ain't my daddy. If I pass on the road and see you laying in a gully dying, I'll pass on by like I don't even know you and let you die!" Me being the baby, I could get away with anything, but even after I got grown. Tootie and Cecil-David thought he'd sic the Cu-Kluk-Clan on me, but he didn't. I didn't care. Something had a-holt'a me. Mama'd say, real quite, "Don't do evil for evil, baby. When somebody do you evil, do 'em good." But I knowed her heart...or thought I did...'til one day she told me I had ways just like him. I'm shamed to even repeat what I said to my mama. I know I hurt her to her heart cause she just left me to God then. The Bible tell you not to cuss your mama...and your daddy...or your lamp be put out in everlasting darkness. That's why I stays in this room, guess I'm just waiting for the lamp to go out...'cause God don't like ugly. He just don't!

ADDIE: [*Quietly, respecting* **GOLDIE***'s mood.*] Ain't this something?! I won that recitation prize in high school, doing a Langston Hughes poem on this very thing...
>   "My old man was a White old man
>   And my old mama was Black.
>   If ever I cursed my White old man
>   I take my curses back.

If ever I cursed my Black old mother
And wished her soul in hell
I'm sorry for the things I said
And now I wish them well."

[**GOLDIE** *weeps quietly.* **ADDIE** *kisses the top of her Aunt's head and then enfolds her lovingly in her arms.*]

ADDIE: Aw, Aunt Goldie, they forgive you...both of 'em forgive you...I know they do.

[*Curtain.*]

★

scene from
LEFT SHOE'S BUDDY
by J. e. Franklin

_____

LEFT SHOE: And spend the rest-a your life in the penten'tia? Cause if you cross state lines with that pistol, Wolfie, they gonna throw the book at you.

WOLFIE: I don't care no more.

LEFT SHOE: Well, what about me. How you think I'm gonna feel knowing you locked up for life and I can't do nothing to help you get out?

WOLFIE: How much life do I have left in this world, anyhow?

LEFT SHOE: I shore can't tell you that, Wolfie, 'cause I don't even know how much time I got left. But if I had took a life which I didn't put in this world, I'd spend the rest-a whatever time I had left making up for the life I had took, and that would keep me pretty busy 'til my own time was up.

WOLFIE: I was trying to raise little Peanut...[*A beat.*] I didn't wanna kill that fellow. I wasn't nothing but a kid then...22-years-old...but I was married to my first wife. Different peoples had been telling me when I'd go to work, this man would come to the house but I could never catch him at it. One time he gived her some money to keep for him. She said he told her it was for her, so she spent it, see? He come to the house to get the money one day and she didn't have it and he jumped on her, beat her all in her face, stomped her and broke her ribs, had her bottom lip hanging all down on her chin...she was carrying my kid or so she said it was mine. I went down to where I knowed he hung out, down at the Do-Drop-Inn...told him I just wanted to talk to him. I wasn't knowed to carry no gun or knife nothing, so he walked on out the place with me. We went into this alley-way and he say, "I know what you wanna talk about." He ain't acted like he was sorry for what he did or nothing, and that made me madder. I was walking a little piece in front-a him and I swung around and hit him so hard with my fist one-a his eyeballs came out. He went down like he was dead but he wasn't...[*A beat as* **LEFT SHOE** *listens.*] I grabbed both-a his legs and spread 'em open, and then I stomped all up in him...tore him all up. Tears was running all down my face til the front-a my shirt was soaking wet. I was just-a kicking and trembling and crying til I couldn't do it no mo'. He didn't die til about two days later. That's when the sheriff come for me. I was working in this blacksmith shop at the time, making horseshoes. I seen the sheriff come in and I didn't run...just kept on working. He say, "I come to take you in, Julius." I say, "I know...but I ain't going." "Come on, now," he says. "The peoples done sent me to git you and I gotta take you." I say just like I said the first time, "I ain't going." He pulled out his pistol. "Don't make me have to shoot you, Julius." "Go'on shoot me!" I says. "That's just what you gonna have'ta do, 'cause I ain't going nowhere with you." His hand commence to trembling, and he put the pistol back in his holster and says, "All right, Julius. I'm going back and tell the peoples what happened and if they send me back here and say I gotta take you in, it's gonna be woe-be-unto you." And he left, but he never did come back, 'cause it was told to me that the higher up peoples and the judge told 'em to let me alone, 'cause they found out why I had did what I did. I stayed there in that place about another three months...nobody wouldn't have nothing to do with me. They kept-a pointing at me and calling me Cain and such as that and mess like "Yonder go a murderer," and asking me "How do it feel to me a murderer?" and such as that. I told 'em "How you think it feel? How you think it feel if I muck you up?" Finally I just left! [*A beat.*]

LEFT SHOE: I never killed nobody...not even when I was in the service.

WOLFIE: I don't wanna kill nobody else...but this wench...! Wasn't enough she done took every stick-a furniture...had me coming home and the place so empty I could hear my own echo...but I found out them papers she had me signing wasn't no 'doption papers on Little Peanut like she told me they was. They was to get a damn credit card in my name, and now her and that boy going all cross the country charging gas and motel rooms and got them people calling here about the money.

LEFT SHOE: Wolfie, I told you, come to that program and take up reading and writing with me.

WOLFIE: I didn't want nobody to know I couldn't do it.

★

scene from
LONG TIME SINCE YESTERDAY
by P. J. Gibson

Born in Pittsburgh, Pennsylvania and raised in Trenton, New Jersey, P. J. Gibson holds an M.F.A. in Theatre Arts from Brandeis University and a B.A. in Drama, Religion and English from Keuka College.

Ms. Gibson began her writing career at the age of nine. To date she has written twenty-six plays which have received thirty-four productions. She also has numerous poems and short stories to her credit. She has been the recipient of many honors including a Shubert Fellowship for the study of dramatic writing, a playwriting grant from the National Endowment for the Arts and two prestigious Audelco Awards for *Long Time Since Yesterday*. Her plays and poetry performances have been presented throughout the United States, Europe and Africa.

In addition to being a writer, Ms. Gibson is an Assistant Professor of English at John Jay College of Criminal Justice. There, she teaches Literature, English and Creative Writing courses. She teaches playwriting at Playwrights Horizons in New York City and the Bushfire Theatre in Philadelphia. Ms. Gibson also teaches Theatre, English and Film related courses for the summer session at the University of California at Berkeley.

Ms. Gibson is currently working on a novel entitled *Neidyana* and a collection of erotic short stories. She has also applied her talents to the silver screen, having written a screenplay for Bill Cosby.

Ms. Gibson's published works include *Long Time Since Yesterday* (Samuel French), *Brown Silk and Magenta Sunsets* in the *9 Plays By Black Women* anthology (New American Library), and *Konvergence* in the *New Plays For The Black Theatre* anthology (Third World Press).

[*Lights rise on* JANEEN.]

JANEEN: I'd like to close my eyes and sleep right through all of this. [*Lights dim on* JANEEN.]

LAVEER: It was as though there was more than desire behind her words, there was the sense of decision. I couldn't shake that sound. Caused me to reroute my ticket and book myself on the first flight coming here. Too late...

BABBS: You tried.

LAVEER: I wonder if they give Brownie points in heaven to all the people who "tried" but didn't succeed. [BABBS *refills her brandy snifter.*] Ahh, enough of that. When did all this heavy drinking start?

BABBS: We TV world people live highly stressed lives. It's par for the course. [*She drinks.*]

LAVEER: You're going to end up with cirrhosis of the liver.

BABBS: So I get cirrhosis of the liver.

LAVEER: [*Pause.*] What are you doing to yourself?

BABBS: What am I doing to myself? What haven't I done?...I'm thirty-seven, single, divorced, lonely and stuck in a rut. Great subject for a Sunday evening special, hosted by...Babbs Wilkerson! [*In her anchor person voice.*] Good evening. Babbs Wilkerson. Our topic for the evening "Where are the men of the 'Sixties'?" or...[*In her normal voice.*] "God, I'd just love to run up on one of those fine, spirited, driven, dreamin', doin', basketball playin', DeBois readin', rhythm and blues lovin', nation buildin', woman lovin' 'Brothers of the 'Sixties'." [*To* LAVEER.] Long on the title huh? [*Pause.*] I'm still in love with Frank. How many years is it now? And I'm still in love with him.

LAVEER: Ever thought of seeing him? It would save your liver.

BABBS: I did. About a year ago. You know what I found out? I'm not really in love with Frank, but I'm in love with that New York Harlem Frank he was in the sixties. Remember the sixties? I'm hooked on midnight navy blue Black, six four, suave talking, intelligent, pretty teeth, good kissing, fine loving, "I'm going to be somebody," nation building, brothers of the sixties. I'm hooked. Shit!...Try to find one today. [*Enter* THELMA *and* PANZI.]

THELMA: Try to find one of what today?

LAVEER: The brothers from the sixties.

THELMA: Who's looking for the brothers from the sixties?

BABBS: I am. [*To* **LAVEER.**] I did a special on our penal system about a year ago. My way of finding out just how many of our men are rotting away in there. You wouldn't believe. Fine ones, kind ones, shy ones...

PANZI: Sounds like a song to me.

BABBS: Okay...Laugh it off but...they're in there, all kinds of charges; nickel bags, subversion, being a Panther, being a friend of a Panther. All these fine brothers from the sixties behind bars, my heart...

THELMA: [*Softly to* **LAVEER.**] How'd we get on this?

LAVEER: Frank.

BABBS: You know, I felt good about myself in the sixties. The brothers were men. You didn't have to worry about the color of your skin.

PANZI: She's rhyming again.

BABBS [*She drinks.*] Damn I miss the sixties [*To* **THELMA.**] How you ever missed the spirit of the sixties is still beyond me. And the men...the confidence, drive, determination. That stuff moved mountains. Damn the seventies and eighties...everything's changed. Look at Frank. He's complacent. Harlem, revolutionary Frank...I need me a man with a mixture, you know? A street wise, book wise, cognac and Budweiser mixture. [*Pause.*] You think I'll find that in Minneapolis? Maybe I ought to buy a home in Dorchester and work in a community center.

THELMA: Now I know she's drunk.

BABBS: I beg your pardon. I am not drunk. [*Crossing to* **THELMA**.] Tell me something Thelma...now stop me if you think I'm getting out of line but...you know I always thought you were a beautiful woman. I know what you think, and I think you have a piss poor opinion of your God given...[*Thinks.*] Attributes.

LAVEER: Come on Babbs, let's go out on the porch for a little air.

BABBS: I don't need any air...[*To* **THELMA**.] I'm really confused about some things...and I don't mean to offend you...

LAVEER: Come on Babbs.

BABBS: I told you, I don't need no air! [*To* **THELMA**.] Where was I? Oh yeah...How did you make it through the sixties and not come out with a better way of feeling about yourself? That was the dawn of *Essence*. How'd you do it? Dark clothes, thick glasses, corner of the room...I mean that was the time to step forward and shine and you stepped backwards and hid. Why? [*Silence.*] Would it be too much to ask for an answer?

THELMA: [*Silence.*] You want an answer? I don't have one. What do you expect? Why is the sky blue? Why is one child to healthy parents born brilliant while the other retarded? I don't know. You understand? You met my sister, Ava, my brothers, James and Dawson...You get a good look at them? Hum?...Could have come from your family, right? Now you look at me. Get yourself a good look at me. [*Pause.*] In my house, my family...my people ooh and ahh when a baby is born with light eyes, light hair and God bless the lightest skin possible, your skin...

BABBS: That doesn't say your brothers and sister are more beautiful because...

THELMA: You did not grow up in my house! You understand? You did not live through the subtleties. I did. I had to be better than everyone. Become a doctor. Did they?...You don't shake that kind of pain over night. Neither you, the sixties, Martin Luther,

Stokely, Rap, Malcolm or a new make over...[*Indicates her face.*] is going to change what I feel. You don't think I've tried? My mirrors don't reflect back the same reflection as yours.

BABBS: It's not suppose to.

THELMA: In my world it is. Now if that sounds sick, it sounds sick and you'll pardon me if it takes me a little longer to work this thing through. Who knows, I might surprise you. Wake up one morning healed, like in a "Hands On" service. But right now...I don't want to talk about it, especially to you. [*She crosses to the door.*] Now, if you don't mind, I'll excuse myself for a little of this northern porch sitting. Maybe the east wind will cleanse me, heal me. I might even return glowing with whatever it is you'd like me to have, but right now I need some air. [*She exits.*]

BABBS: [*Silence.*] Well...I guess I fucked up that time, didn't I? Guess this is giving me a bit of cirrhosis of the brain. [*She places the brandy snifter on the table.*] Now to eat crow and beg her forgiveness. [*She crosses to the door and exits. Silence.*]

★

scene from
LONG TIME SINCE YESTERDAY
by P. J. Gibson

PANZI: Janeen was a woman.

ALISA: And you used her.

PANZI: No, you used her! All of you used her. In your own little blood sucking ways you used her "innocence" "naivete." Janeen wanted to be a woman. She wasn't weak, vulnerable, innocent or naive. She was a woman finding her own.

THELMA: And you helped her.

PANZI: I gave her what she wanted and needed.

LAVEER: You pain't a revealing portrait except you negate the true colors, the blacks and grays...You asked what we talked about during her last week. You. Sometimes two, three times a day. You. Your distance. Her feeling of being conquered. Where were you? Too busy living?

PANZI: I'm suppose to be the bad guy because I care about my relationship with Arlene?

LAVEER: Janeen had a relationship, a husband, Walter, or have you forgotten?

PANZI: I never asked her to change her life. I never suggested she leave Walter.

LAVEER: What a shame you never sat her down and taught her the rules. Let me fill you in on something. That Sunday, while you were up there rolling around in the sheets...[*She indicates upstairs.*] After Walter got a bird's eye view of the two of you, he went off. Chose a Sunday and went off, raped her. Later giving her the motive, a vivid account of what he had seen.

ALISA: No.

LAVEER: Then, two weeks ago, after telling him she was pregnant...[**PANZI** *is shocked by this news.*] I'm not surprised you didn't know. But she was. And guess how Walter viewed the baby? Guess?!!!! Something you couldn't give her.

ALISA: Oh God...

LAVEER: Do you know how many lives you've screwed? Do you know what you did to that man? You don't care, do you? I know, I've been watching you. Trying to understand, put the pieces together. It's never been about Janeen, has it? Looking back over the years, you know what I see?

PANZI: I could give a damn about what you see,

LAVEER: Give a damn. You give a damn. Janeen is laying out there in a plot of Ewing Cemetery. You damn well better give a damn.

PANZI: Or what?!

LAVEER: Winning!!!...All about winning. Graduation day, Janeen gave me an ultimatum concerning our friendship. You motivated that, orchestrated it. Years of friendship down the drain and why?...Pawns...rooks, kings, queens...It was too much Janeen and I had become friends again. You had to top that, had to win. Well you won! You won! How's the victory feel Panzi?!!! Tell me, how's the victory?

THELMA: STOP IT!!! JESUS GOD!!!...PLEASE!!!!...Please... [*Silence.*] What's happened to us? Will somebody please tell me what's happened to us? Look at us. Listen to us. All those years of dreaming...The places we thought we'd be, things we thought we'd be doing...And what have we become? Drunks, dykes, nonconformists, crusaders, hiders...[*She crosses to* **PANZI.**] What you did was wrong. There's no debate on the subject. What you did Jansen...What you do is wrong. It defies what we stood for. It defies the laws of nature, the laws of God and when you defy the laws of God—

PANZI:—Don't you preach to me about God. I know about God and his laws.

THELMA: Do tell...What God?

PANZI: Your God, a God who abandons...And one of his laws in particular...Exodus twenty, twelve. You know it?

THELMA: I'm not up to game playing with you, Panzi.

PANZI: No game playing. Your God set out a law; "Honor thy father and thy mother that thy..."

THELMA: Watch it, you're on the edge of being sacrilegious.

PANZI: [*To* **THELMA.**] "That thy days may be long upon the land which the Lord the God giveth thee" Some law...Seems to me your God forgot an important one "Parent, honor and love thy children that they may not know pain, may not know hurt, may not be neglected." [*To* **ALISA.**] You understand the need for that one, don't you Alisa? [*To* **THELMA.**] Did your God simply forget to add this or did it simply not matter? [*To* **ALISA.**] Do you think you were the only child on this green earth to suffer in youth? You don't hold a patent on it! All of us don't grow up to be quite so sanctimonious and perfect!

ALISA: I'm sure...

PANZI: No! I have the floor! My turn!...I was born the soul daughter of Adrelline Lucinda McVain. A very beautiful shapely, silky hair Adrelline Lucinda McVain. A woman known for her knowledge of beauty secrets...jewelry. [*She directs 'jewelry' to* **LAVEER**.] A mother of three; two boys and one girl. A woman who loved men almost as much as her reflection in the mirror. She had to have her ego stroked continually, had to have euphoric adulations gracing her ears never endingly. My mother...She had four husbands. All legal. Discarded them when they ran out of adjectives to describe her beauty. I used to wonder if she'd divorce me one day, discard me. I had nightmares of my brothers coming down to the breakfast table and finding my chair vacant and Momma explaining in her sweet sultry voice...Panzi didn't know how to talk to Momma. Momma don't share her roof with nobody who don't know how to talk to Mamma.' We'd heard that many times; after Daddy disappeared, after Daddy Rudolph, Daddy Jimmy, Daddy Mason...My brothers, they learned early, caught on quickly, how to talk and stroke Momma. They'd hug her, kiss her, stroke her ego...and she'd repay you well for flattery. Buy you...presents...All you had to do was be a man and know how to compliment Momma...[*To* **ALISA**.] And you talk of innocence. When my flat chest began to grow, Momma's eyes got colder, her words more bitter. There was no room for a girl child in my Momma's house...When I was nine, I asked Momma for a Susie Walkmate Doll. It was the only thing I wanted for Christmas. I did everything just the way Momma liked them done to get that doll, [*Pause*.] Christmas Eve morning Momma got a phone call. I knew it was from a man because she took a long lavender perfume bath after she hung up the phone. She put on her make-up, her satin robe with the fuzzy feathers, her pink high heel slippers...I knew it was a man by the way her eyes bit into me. I hid when Mr. Jones rang the door bell. I held my head low when he gave my brothers and me presents. I tried to disappear when he told Momma I was growing into a beautiful young lady, I prayed Mr. Jones hadn't messed things up. Christmas morning...No Susie Walkmate. Her excuse, the store had run out...Momma never held me. On her dying bed in Mercy Hospital, she clutched my brothers' heads to her breast but never looked at me with those eyes...[*To* **LAVEER**.] Your eyes. [*To* **THELMA**.] Where was your God and

his laws then? Your God did not soothe me. A woman soothed
me. She put her arms around me one cool winter evening while I
was still young and she loved me, made me feel like I belonged in
this world. A woman gave me that. [*To* **LAVEER**.] And
Janeen...That Sunday morning...She needed these hands...I
understood her. I knew her longing. I'd been there. [*She fights
tears*.] I didn't plan for things to...Why did you have to come
back, stir up all the needs, desires, longings for...replicas?...At
first, it was only friendship I needed, but the more you rejected,
the more I wanted and...You became my sickness. Why couldn't
you have just stayed...You had to conjure up all that wanting,
needing, rejecting...Cut from the same cloth...That same beauty,
same cutting edge. You and Momma...Tell me Laveer, what was
wrong with me? What was wrong with me?!!!

LAVEER: Nothing...I simply don't like you,

★

scene from
MY MARK, MY NAME
by P.J. Gibson

Dedicated to George Houston Bass who comissioned this play in
1978.

The young **PHILLIS** wears her freedom like a badge of
honor. From time to time she pulls her manumission paper from her
bosom, waving it in validation of her freedom. **NUBA BRIGGS**, who
has fought on the battlefields and has learned the true meaning of
freedom and being a man, snatchers her freedom paper, crushes it,
throws it to the ground and then says: "Now how free you be?"
My Mark, My Name is a two act realistic drama based on the
historical data of the First Black Regiment of Rhode Island. It is set
in Newport, Rhode Island between the years of 1776 and 1783. The
work addresses the world which stands before the freed Black men
and women after the Revolutionary War. It is a time where freedom
does not mean security and it is a world where a slave, in the midst of
freed Black men, must make a dramatic move in order to gain his
freedom.

SCENE: The BRIGG'S home, Newport, Rhode Island NUBA BRIGG'S (mid 30'S), as well as CEFAR (50), TIVER (early 20's) and JUPITER (late 20's) are "free" Black men and women.

TIME: August 1783.

PHILLIS: What's happened?!!...Oh, no, God...Old Man Stephens done sold my uncle.

CEFAR: He ain't sell Sippeo.

NUBA: Ain't nobody been sold, least wise not yet.

TIVER: Then what's happened?

JUPITER: Nuba ain't goin'.

TIVER: Ain't goin' where?

CEFAR: To Ebibiman.

TIVER: [*To* NUBA.]What you mean you ain't goin'?

NUBA: I feel it's the right thing for me to do.

JUPITER: Right?!! There ain't no right. You ain't got no rights.

NUBA: Then I gotta stay, so as there will be some, at least for the rest of us to come.

JUPITER: That's fine talk, but it's stupid talk. What's stayin' here gonna do for you? You can't be a man here.

NUBA: I ain't in the mood for no more persuasion talk. A man has to do what he feels is right. [*Silence.*]

CEFAR: You know last night I had a dream, 'bout what the belly a those ships musta been like packed with Blacks to be slaves.

Dreamed they all had wheels on they heads, like hats. Big round wheels that these White mens had put on them. The ship come up to a land, this land. The Whites rolled the Blacks out by the wheels on they heads. Rolled them down the planks, one after the other, down the planks, 'round the land...When they stood 'em up, the Blacks, they got to walkin' all crazy...They Black heads still spinnin', eyes searchin' for somethin' constant to latch on to. They were thousands of these mens walkin' 'round in a dizzy. Then I saw one, one man over in the corner. He up and run into a wall and broke his wheel. A White man come up, pushed him down and tried to make him roll, but the man's wheel were broken, and the fall made the wheel fall all the way off. He stood up, the Black man, he stoop up and looked 'round him at all the Blacks, wheels on they heads, movin' 'round in a dizzy. Then the Black man, the one without the wheel on his head...He come up face to face, eye to eye with the White man and saw the world as the White man see it. Then he saw the world as it really be. He got to actin' crazy, breakin' the wheels on the heads of the Black mens. Some resisted, others let
they wheel come up off they head. Then there stood a line, a whole group of Black men like the first, standing face to face, eye to eye with the White man.

PHILLIS: How'd it end Cefar?

CEFAR: These Black men, without the wheels 'round they head, standin' up straight, they walked past the White man and sailed his ship away.

JUPITER: We gonna have to hurry up and get Cefar on that boat. [**PHILLIS** and **JUPITER** laugh.]

NUBA: You're sayin' I got a wheel on my head.

CEFAR: No, your wheel fell off.

NUBA: But...

CEFAR: No buts, I just had a dream.

monologue from
WALK IN DARKNESS
by William Hairston

ROACH: I'm going to marry her, sir. I'm happy...*[Rising from the bench and moving down right of stage.]* for once in my life, and I'm not going to give that up. Nobody can make me give it up. All my natural life people have taken things from me. *[ROACH turns and crosses back to bench and sits.]* First the boys at school, then older people, White and Black. Whenever I had a hold of something I wanted...it was taken right out of my hands, as if I had no right to it. *[ROACH no longer tries to contain his emotions.]* I...I can't explain it clearly...but even my parents pitched in. When I earned money they took it away from me...every Saturday night. They took it whether they needed it or not. And it's been the same with everything...People always telling me where I can go and where I can't, what I can't have and what I can. Now...here I am again. *[Rising and crossing down right of stage.]* And I'm fed up to my neck. Nobody is going to take this from me. Nobody!

[CHAPLAIN: *[Deep with concern]* I understand how you feel.]

ROACH: *[Turning and moving back to right of table.]* I know exactly what's going on. The brass don't give a good goddam whether—*[Embarrassed.]* Oh...I'm sorry, Father.

[CHAPLAIN: Go on.]

ROACH: They don't care if Eva was Nazi or not. And they say they are protecting me. That's a laugh. They've never protected me up to now. I know what they're protecting—a White girl from a Negro, that's all. But the're sadly mistaken this time...because they're going to get another half-White baby...and this half-White baby is going to have a name—my name! *[ROACH sits on the bench again.]* Now, I don't give a damn...*[Catching himself.]* Sorry, Father...*[The CHAPLAIN nods in assurance.]*...if I regret it later. The White soldiers do a lot of things they regret later, and nobody pays any attention. They can raise all the hell they want to...and nobody gives a damn. Well, this time I'm going to raise some hell—I'm getting married! [*Rising.*] You can help me if you want to, Father...but if you don't it won't make any difference...I'm doing it anyways. [*Taking his cap from the table.*] Good night, Father...and thanks. [**ROACH** *turns and crosses off down right.*]

★

Scene from
WALK IN DARKNESS
by William Hairston

_____

ROACH: [*Voice off stage.*] It's me...Washington.

EVA: Kommen sie herein.

[**EVA** *turns and crosses to table and puts the candle on it.* **ROACH** *enters from down stage left. They meet each other and embrace and kiss.*]

ROACH: I'm sorry I woke you.

EVA: [*Concerned.*] What do you do here, Washington?

ROACH: I came to see you...what else?

EVA: [*With fear.*] The police soldats were twice here today for you. They come back any moment. [**ROACH** *crosses to stage right and looks off, then turns and crosses back to* **EVA.**]

ROACH: I won't stay long. I came to see if you were all right.

EVA: Everything is bad. Poppa and Mama called away twice by police soldats. They say you run away from camp. Why do they look for you so much? Why do they not like you any more?

ROACH: [*Sarcastically.*] Because...I'm a bad boy.

EVA: Why you bad boy?

ROACH: Because I married you, that's why. [*They embrace and kiss passionately.*] Let's go to the upstairs window so I can keep an eye outside.

EVA: Nein. You will wake Poppa and Mama. They will not let you get away. They will turn you to the police soldats. They not like what you do.

ROACH: I couldn't help it, they forced my hand.

EVA: Father Durant come, too. He said it is best you report to camp. We cannot live here longer if you run away. All the week come police soldats to ask for you.

ROACH: I can't go back. Not now. I'm too far gone. But you don't have to worry. Everything is going to be all right. I've made some contacts, and I'll be settled in a day so.

EVA: Will you go to America soon now?

ROACH: I'm afraid I won't be going back home for a long time.

EVA: [*Confused.*] You not? Why you not go back now you run from camp?

ROACH: Honey...don't you see? I can't go back to America now... after this. I would be court martialed the minute I set foot on ground.

EVA: [*Disappointedly.*] You do not want to go to your home.

ROACH: [*Appeasingly.*] Sure. I want to go back...but I can't. Not now, anyway.

EVA: Father Durant right. He said it is best you go back to camp.

ROACH: [*Crossing right of center.*] Ah, Eva, honey...can't you see I can't go back to camp either? Once a soldier goes over the hill he's sunk. [*Bitterly.*] I can't go back...not without killing every M.P. in the frigging Army. [ROACH *rubs his hand over his face.* EVA *now notices his condition. She crosses to him.*]

EVA: [*Touching his face.*] Are you hurt, Washington?

ROACH: [*Turning from her.*] It's nothing now. I'm all right.

EVA: You fight with the police soldats?

ROACH: [*Pointedly.*] I'm okay. [EVA *crosses up and sits on bench near table.*]

EVA: Washington...what we do when baby come? [ROACH *crosses to* EVA *and sits on bench.*]

ROACH: By that time I'll be rich. It's only about four months off. Everything will be all right. Take my word for it. Have you got enough food left?

EVA: You not bring food in long time. You bring something?

ROACH: Not this time. I'm afraid things will be a little hard for a while. I'll try and bring something soon, though.

EVA: [*Concerned.*] Do not come again.

ROACH: How am I going to get you food?

EVA: You bring us all to jail.

ROACH: Okay. I'll try and send it to you. [*Concerned for her.*]

How do you feel?

EVA: [*Shrugging her shoulders, and rising.*] Bad. All the time I am sick. I think you go now. [*She takes his arm.*] We wake Poppa and Mama.

ROACH: So what...?

EVA: They not let you get away. You do not know what you do to us. [*Turning from him.*] Whole village is against us. Everyone.

ROACH: [*Rising.*] Don't let these villagers upset you. People never do what they can to help. They just like to sit around and look...and talk about you.

EVA: [*Crossing to left of table.*] I was by Frau Doerr yesterday. She have much yarn for knitting. Always she give me some for cigarettes.

ROACH: The woman that runs the cat-house down the road?

EVA: [*Not comprehending.*] Kaat house...?

ROACH: Never mind. Forget it.

EVA: Frau Doerr now says she have no yarn for the Black baby.

ROACH: [*Banging on the table.*] The bitch!

EVA: The women who live by Frau Doerr, they tell her she must say that: "No yarn for the Black baby."

ROACH: [*Turning on EVA.*] I heard you the first time! A drop of Negro blood makes him Black...eh...? [*Trying to control himself.*] What did you say to her?

EVA: Nothing. What could I say?

ROACH: Are you worried about the baby being Black?

EVA: [*Shrugging shoulders the crossing to ROACH.*] Baby could be. I do not care.

ROACH: Who gives a damn if it's Black or White. It'll be a human being, won't it?
EVA: Yes...but the people do not know that.

ROACH: [*Moving back from EVA.*] To hell with them! Are you ashamed of having a baby by me?

EVA: [*Crossing to ROACH.*] But the people talk. You know how the people talk.

ROACH: [*Turning from EVA with anger.*] I don't give a goddam what they do...these lousy sons-of-bitches. Do they think they're better than we are? [ROACH *crosses to stage left, and turns to the audience.*] I ought to go out there and smash her skull in—that Doerr bitch. That'll fix her catting game good and proper. I'm not taking any crap from a lousy Nazi bitch.

EVA: Frau Doerr was not Nazi.

ROACH: To hell with her. But if this lousy village sits around talking like lunatics...goddam it...I'll kill them. [EVA *crosses to* ROACH.]

EVA: Do not be angry, Washington. I do not care about the people. I want the baby...even if it is Black.

ROACH: [*Turning on EVA.*] Oh, you do, do you that's mighty nice of you. I'm flattered all to hell!

EVA: Important is that we love each other. You are big and strong. You protect me.

ROACH: Who says you need protection? [**ROACH** *crosses to right of stage.*] You're not an invalid who has to sit around and feel sorry for yourself. You said in the very beginning you wanted the baby.

EVA: I do want baby from you.

ROACH: [*Calming down.*] Well...don't get all worked up about people. You can't understand this kind of situation...but I've had to live with it all my life.

EVA: [*Crossing to* **ROACH.**] But did you not know it would be bad for me here? The people are stupid. Stupid and evil.

ROACH: I know. I know.

EVA: Even Doktor Habicht is evil. I was by him yesterday.

ROACH: I suppose he won't bring a black baby into the world.

EVA: [*Shaking her head.*] Nein. Only he said, "Frau Roach, you man is American. Go to military hospital."

ROACH: [*Holding her.*] All right, forget about him. You go to the best doctor in Munich.

EVA: [*Exhaling in despair.*] I think you better go before police soldats come again.

ROACH: I guess maybe you're right. [*Taking* **EVA**'s *hands.*] Now don't worry about anything...and try not to bother the villagers for anything. You hear?

EVA: I hear, Washington.

ROACH: I'll send you some food soon...and cigarettes so you can buy some of the other things you need. I'll try to get some yarn too. [*He starts off left but stops and turns to* EVA.] And listen...when I send the stuff to you, you'll have a letter written for me. That's the way we'll keep in contact with each other. [*He turns and starts off again but stops.*] Is the back door locked?

EVA: Yes.

ROACH: [*Crossing back to* EVA.] That's okay. I'll crawl out the basement window. [ROACH *pulls some bills from his pocket and gives some to* EVA.] This'll have to do until I send something. [ROACH *crosses off down right and exits.* EVA *takes the candle from the table and exits up stage left.*

★

scene from
AMERI/CAIN GOTHIC
by Paul Carter Harrison

Playwright/Director Paul Carter Harrison is a New York
native whose plays have been published and produced in Europe and
around the United States. The NEC has produced *The Great
MacDaddy* in 1974 for which he was awarded an Obie Award; and
Abercrombie Apocalypse in 1982. Other significant works produced in
New York include his multi-media drama, *The Death of Boogie
Woogie* at the Richard Allen Cultural Center in 1980; the musico-
epic, *Tabernacle*, at the Afro-American Studio Theatre in 1981 for
which he won an Audelco Award; and *Ameri/Cain Gothic* at the New
Federal Theatre in 1985.

He is also the author of *The Drama of Nommo* (1973), a
collection of essays that examines the retention of Africanisms in the
American experience that informs the aesthetics of Black Theatre;
and the editor of *Kuntu Drama* (1974), an anthology of African
diaspora plays; and *Totem Voices* (1984), an anthology of plays from
the Black World Repertory (all by Grove Press). In addition, he is the
author of the text for Charles Stewart's *Jazz File* (1985), a photo
documentary published by Little Brown and Company, and the Bert
Andrews photo book on Black Theatre, *In The Shadow of the Great
White Way* (1989, Thunder's Mouth Press). He has also been a
Contributing and Advisory Editor for *Callaloo Magazine* (1985-
1988). A recipient of the Rockefeller Foundation fellowship for
American Playwriting, he currently serves as Writer-in-Residence at
Columbia College (Chicago) where he has developed the libretto for
his recent jazz inspired operettas: *Anchorman* and *Goree Crossing*.

HARPER: Give yourself to Jesus!

CASS: And I was full of Christ. I had nothing to fear.

HARPER: [HARPER *begins to sermonize in a tone redolent of a
used-car salesman.*] Now, my friends, I know that some of you are
thinking that you've gotta have luck to get along in this world.
Many of you, right this very moment, are carrying a rabbit's foot
in your purses, or wearing a four-leaf clover in your hair. Some of
you even have significant numbers written on your sleeves, while
others sleep at night with a special button, a stick-pin, some kinda

lode stone under their pillows. Well, you wouldn't need to covet all that junk, friends, if you'd come into the ministry and give yourself to Jesus. You can turn it all in, right here, like you would an old Chevy, then walk outta here with a spankin' new soul. You can't play Jesus cheap, Friends. He's got a better deal for each and every man or woman, rich or poor. I'm reminded of that old Invitational anthem...!
[*He turns around to face* **CASS** *upstage who sings the chorus section of the* Pilgrim Invitational Hymn *which is now highly audible.*]

CASS: [*Greatly animated.*]
O wandering souls! Come near me.
My sheep should never fear me.
I am the Shepherd true.
I am the Shepherd true.
[**HARPER** *resumes the sermon as* **CASS** *mutters responses intermittently. The* Invitational Hymn *ends.*]

HARPER: Now, such a little daughter is on her way to becoming a godly woman. We can hear about a beautiful woman anytime. Even a smart woman. Or a career woman. Maybe even a talented woman. But we seldom ever hear the good news about a godly woman. I'm talkin' about the true keepers of the Spring. [**CASS** *slaps her hands joyously above her head, clasps them, and slowly brings them down, making a transition from joy to sorrow.*]

HARPER: [*Continued.*] She was lackin' spiritual exercise, and her soul had become soft and flabby. This gal needed help badly. So when she heard about the wonderful power of our Spiritual Leader, she decided to come amongst the crowd and test him. Folks always wanna test a good product before they use it. Now, as the Spiritual Leader came down that desolate street, and through that massive crowd, this woman, with tears in her eyes, and her righteous name on her lips, reached out to touch him. [**CASS** *gestures toward him, then throws herself down at his feet.*]

HARPER: [*Continued.*] But where...? On his head would be too irreverent, and his hand, much to familiar. She angled down at the hem of his robe. [**CASS** *touches* **HARPER** *at the ankle and reacts with spontaneous bliss while kneeling.* **HARPER** *turns around suddenly.*]

HARPER: [*Continued.*] Who touched me...? Remember, he said, who touched me? Then looked down at his hem-line to witness the magnetic effects of faith. [**HARPER** *helps* **CASS** *to her feet. She turns around, slowly walks to the bed, allowing her housecoat to fall to the floor, then climbs onto the bed, and rocks back 'n forth on her knees reverently. The muted sound of the* Pilgrim Invitational Hymn *is heard from the box.*]

HARPER: [*Continued.*] He reached down and touched the woman benevolently 'side her cheek. And lo and behold, grace had come to that woman. The lines that marred her beauty were gone, and her body was released from pain. New life had come to that woman's body. She was a sanctified woman. A godly woman. Let us pray...! Lord Jesus, we come to Thee now as little children. Dress us again in clean pinafores. Make us tidy once more with the tidiness of true remorse and confession. Oh, wash our hearts, that they may be clean again. Make us to know the strengthening joys of the Spirit, and the newness of life which only Thee can give. Amen! [*Sound of the* **TRANSITOR VOICE** *as lights return to normal.*]

[**TRANSITOR VOICE:** Home to Harper...! Home callin' Harper...! Come on in, Harper...!]

★

scene from
DEATH OF BOOGIE WOOGIE
by Paul Carter Harrison

[**MOON** sings *Blues-ballad as* **SUNNY** *crosses behind* **SPIDER** *and* **CHOCOLATE CHIP** *to reach her;* **CLAYBORNE** *joins the tableau.*]

MOON:
What is there to do
   when the hand goes 'round the clock
   and the love you had has stopped
but stew
   your own brew
Sugar.

There is nothin' left to do
   when the love you found at home
   is like a cupboard without a bone
but stew
   your own brew
Sugar.

Stew your own brew
and take like anew
cause the worse thing
you can do
Sugar
is cry the Blues
in your stew.

[**MOON** *stirs pot and tastes as* **SUNNY** *enters.*]

SUNNY: How you doin', Sugar? [**MOON** *is surprised to see him. She places spoon in pot and attempts to tidy up her appearance.*]

MOON: Oh, Hi, Sunny! Sorry I look such a mess. Wasn't expectin' no company. Didn't have time to clean up or nothin'!

SUNNY: Don't go through no changes for me, Sugar. I just popped in for a minute.

MOON: Always good to see you, Sunny. You've change a lot. I guess I have too. Don't take care myself like I used to do.

SUNNY: It's been a long time, Moon. But you'll always look good to me.

MOON: Oh, you don't have to say that, Sunny.

SUNNY: I mean it, Sugar!

MOON: Then, where you been hidin? Oh, never mind. You don't have to tell me. You just too busy, that's all. I see you on television a lot. Ain't got nothin' better to do. I guess I could do better if I wasn't so darn tired when I come home from work. And I work hard at my new job, much harder than down at P-U-C. So at night I have nothin' better to do than watch you on the tube. It must be somethin' bein' a star and all, huh, Sunny?

SUNNY: A lotta hard work. And I ain't got nothin' better to do. How long you been livin' here?

MOON: Quite some time, now. Kinda off beaten-path, ain't it? It ain't much, but I'm really quite happy!

SUNNY: Are you really happy, Moon?

MOON: Oh, you know what I mean. You get used to livin' with yourself and you feel quite happy you can do it, you know?

SUNNY: It ain't like you, Moon, bein' cooped up like this on the outskirts of town. Had a hard time finding you. Don't you ever get out?

MOON: Every once and awhile when the weather is good. Don't go to far, though. Just a little stroll in the neighborhood.

SUNNY: You need to get out and have some fun, Moon. Remember the ball we used to have?

MOON: All I need to do is live, Sunny. And I'm doin' that quite nicely, thank you. How 'bout you?

SUNNY: I guess I'm livin' pretty good, now. But it ain't the same without you.

MOON: But you'll get along somehow, won't you? Isn't that what you said when you left me?

SUNNY: You know I didn't mean it, Sugar!

MOON: Not in the beginnin', but in the end you meant every word of it. I'm not even mad about it. Not anymore. But I do remember tryin' to tell you where you were comin' from and where you were goin', and you stuck out your lip and tightened up your jaw and said "I'm tired of hearin' the same old shit!," remember? So I said nothin'! I just looked at you. And when I looked at you too hard, you'd say, "I don't wanna hear no grief this mornin'!" I had nothin' to say. The next day either when you'd poke out your mouth and remind me that you hung out all night and played away your pay and shout, "What you got to say 'bout that?" Nothin'! What was I supposed to say? All I had to do is gaze into your eyes and I could tell you were burnin' up inside. So I grew colder as your smile became a distant breath away when you turned your head to say "stop breathin' down my collar!" unless I was willin' to get an extra job to help you make it. Now, you know I wasn't supposed to say nothin' behind that! Then you finally said it for me, "Don't talk, Sugar, just walk!" And I said nothin'! Not a mumblin' word. Cause you were on the rise and about to be a star. Then you left. Packed up your flame in a samsonite bag and left me alone to watch the world go 'round. And I still ain't got nothin' to say!

SUNNY: I came back, Moon!

MOON: Not to stay! You just popped in for a minute. And it's good to see you, Sunny.

SUNNY: I look all over for you, Moon.

MOON: I died for awhile, but I'm a new Moon now.

SUNNY: I wanna do somethin' for you.

MOON: There's nothin' you can do for me that I can't do for myself, Sunny. So let's just be friends. [*He attempts to kiss her. She resists.*]

MOON: [*Continued.*] Uh-uh, Baby! Not like that! Silver and Gold couldn't buy you this Sugar!

SUNNY: I guess things have changed sho nuff! [**MOON** *tastes Soup in pot.*]

MOON: Like a change in the weather!

SUNNY: I see you still keep your hands in the pots. What's cookin'?

MOON: Bay-leaf soup!

SUNNY: Bay-leaf...?

MOON: Remember how you used to love it?

SUNNY: Then I'd howl at the Moon.

MOON: There's enough here for two. But we'd have to share the bowl.

SUNNY: No thanks, Sugar. I don't think I have the stomach for it anymore.

MOON: [*She sips soup for bowl.*] Only food I ever eat, now.

SUNNY: No wonder you're so pale, Moon. I'm worried about you, really.

MOON: You needn't worry. Bay-leaf sustains my life quite well. It helps me to see things clearly. I see things more clearly than ever before. Sometimes I shouldn't see and it scares me.

SUNNY: You dream too much, Moon, and that's scary. I remember you'd carry your dreams around in a tape-recorder. You would dream with a full orchestra in the background that we were in a Hollywood picture traveling around the world in eighty days to arrive on some deserted ancient corner. Drums would be callin' and we'd answer in unknown tongues, as we crossed the desert on a triple-humped-back Camel in the middle of the sandstorm, singing our way home to Dahomey. [*They begin to sing song.*]

MOON and SUNNY:
When the road gets tough
   and you've had enough
Baby,
   it's time for Hoodoo.
When you've lost your way
   cause you've gone astray
The only thing to do
   is call on Hoodoo
Legba, talk to me
Legba, talk to me
Take me by the hand
   and show me through.

When your love grows cold
   and the rivers in your
   soul won't blow,
Baby,
   it's time for Hoodoo.
When your life looks dim
   at the moment you see
   all your glory end
The only thing to do
   is call on Hoodoo.

Legba, talk to me.
Legba, talk to me.
Take me by the hand
    to Damballah's Kingdom

When you're feelin' Blue
    cause you don't have the world
    that was promised you
Baby,
    it's time for Hoodoo.
When your spirit cries
    for fear that you're
    gonna let it die
The only thing to do
    is call on Hoodoo.
Legba, talk to me
Legba, talk to me
Open up my eyes
    and show me through.
Ooowee! Ooowee!
Ooweewahwahwah
Ooweewahwahwah

[CHAFALFA: [*Looks up from her work as if startled.*] Sunny...?
That you, Sunny Boy?]

SUNNY: I gotta go, Moon.

MOON: Be careful, Sunny. There's some stormy weather
brewing!

SUNNY: I'll live!

★

scene from
CODA
by Bill Harris

WEATHERSPOON: They don't have a clue. [*"To prove my point."*] You know how I got possession of this joint?

MADDOX: [*Surprised that he doesn't. A confession.*] Actually I wasn't that sure you really owned it.

WEATHERSPOON: [*Mild surprise.*] Oh, yeah?

MADDOX: I always assumed you were probably fronting for some white man. Like all the rest of the spooks who were so-called owners.

WEATHERSPOON: Well, at first I was. I was. You were right. Who owned it before me was the gangsters.

MADDOX: Like a Purple Gang gangster?...them kind of gangsters?

WEATHERSPOON: [*"Correct." makes a finger/thumb pistol, aims at* **MADDOX** *and fires.*] What he would do is get a bar in a neighborhood changing from white to colored...Take out a lot of insurance on it, and then eventually burn it down and beat the insurance company, see. See, this wasn't the first place I'd managed for him, see. And he liked me, because I was hip to all the various little tricks the bartenders and waitresses used trying to skim off money: false pockets and all that, and I kept them honest.

MADDOX: [*Knowing better.*] And you wasn't skimming nothing, huh?

WEATHERSPOON: [*"I was, but..."*] I had a family to support—

MADDOX: [*Laughs.*] Okay.

WEATHERSPOON: But I fell in love with this joint the first time I ever set foot in it. I don't know—Wasn't a minute I spent in here I didn't wish it was mine.

MADDOX: Okay.

WEATHERSPOON: You know my daddy got run out of the south.

MADDOX: [*"I'm hip."*] For not letting them crackers ride him like a mule.

WEATHERSPOON: Yeah. And the thing that hurt till the day he died, was he wasn't able to pass a plot of land on to me, like his father done for him. Own some land, that was his song.

MADDOX: My Daddy had a different song.

WEATHERSPOON: Up here it seemed to me like "land" translated into "business." You see what I'm saying?

MADDOX: I hear you.

WEATHERSPOON: And a business was what I wanted to pass on to my sons. But there was no way, on what I was making *and* stealing, I could afford to buy it. So, in the mean time I'm running it for this guy: and at the end of every week he calls me about quitting time and tells me where to meet him and deliver the bag with all the profits for that week. In cash, see.

MADDOX: Northern share-cropping.

WEATHERSPOON: Then, after a while, three or four weeks go by and I don't hear from him. Nothing. Then I get a call and he tells me where to meet him with the money. And not to leave nothing in here the next night I might want the following day.

MADDOX: Uh oh, I smell smoke.

WEATHERSPOON: [*"Exactly."*] What I been most afraid of is about to happen.

MADDOX: Every time.

WEATHERSPOON: 'Cause it suddenly hit me: the minute the match is struck I'm out of work.

MADDOX: But you knew it was coming...

WEATHERSPOON: Sooner or later...But hearing him say it, look like it almost give me my first heart attack.

MADDOX: Getting an honest, nine to five J-O-B ever cross your mind?

WEATHERSPOON: [*Quickly and finally.*] You ever think about going to swing and sway with Sammy Kaye?

MADDOX: Enough said.

WEATHERSPOON: So, that night, I hightail it out there with the sack from the safe. He's no where around. Something's wrong, and I know it. But I wait. See, I knew all along this joint was just a little side operation for this guy. A personal thing aside from his real, big time, gangster business.

MADDOX: It's your livelihood and it ain't nothing but a hobby for him.

WEATHERSPOON: Mainly so he can be around the strippers, you dig.

MADDOX: Pocket change.

WEATHERSPOON: That's right. And suddenly, out of nowhere, there he is.

MADDOX: Your guy. [*Music: Bass walks under the following* *section.*]

WEATHERSPOON: And-he-is-double scared. Then I *knew* something else was happening. I know he, being who he was, wasn't *that* scared of the law, local or federal. In fact, he wasn't the kind of scared you be about money, or doing time—He was scared for his life kind of scared. And I figure there's some double crossing going on somewhere, and it must be his own people that he is that scared of. And for a few minutes we just sit there, like two old maids in church. Nobody saying nothing. Finally I says, real cool, I'm playing it like I'm George Raft, see. I says, How you doing?

MADDOX: Edward G. Robinson is my man.

WEATHERSPOON: "How you doing?," you know, and he says, confidential, the whole nature of his business is about to change in a *big* way and he's got to lay low till he can make it all happen. We sit some more, two old maids, till finally I says, "If there's anything I can do—," just like that, y'know, George Raft.

MADDOX: [*"Sure."*] Cool. It's what you say anyway, to somebody with a problem.

WEATHERSPOON: And he like looked at me like I was Santa Claus and he's three years old.

MADDOX: All because you just said—

WEATHERSPOON: "If there's anything I can do..." For a minute I thought he was going to kiss me. He says he doesn't know why he didn't think of me in the first place; says he knows he can trust me; and right then I was just about the only person he knew who he could trust.

MADDOX: You knew then it was his own people was after him.

WEATHERSPOON: [*"Exactly."*] Said he needed a favor. And he'd pay me what-ever I asked.

MADDOX: The boy was serious.

WEATHERSPOON: As suicide. It was one of those moments, Dox. A classic. I started to say the money that I already had in the sack. But he hadn't mentioned the money...[*Pantomimes clandestinely pushing the money sack out of sight.*]

MADDOX: So you don't. Maybe he's so scared he'll forget it.

WEATHERSPOON: Then I thought I'll ask him for some *different* money.

MADDOX: *He* asked *you*, so wasn't no time for being shy.

WEATHERSPOON: Whatever it is it's got something to do with his life.

MADDOX: So maybe he ain't in no mood to negotiate.

WEATHERSPOON: I don't know if it was then it come to me, or after I had time to think it over, calm: about how he was making money off us on both ends.

MADDOX: While he's in business and afterwards, too. And we end up with the ashes.

WEATHERSPOON: [*"Exactly!"*] And I don't know—But without skipping a beat, I said I'd do what-ever it was, sight unseen...

MADDOX: Un huh?

WEATHERSPOON: For the papers on this joint. And his promise not to burn it down.

MADDOX: The element of surprise. He was expecting you to ask for money. Because they think that's all we're interested in.

WEATHERSPOON: That's right. And I crossed him up.

MADDOX: Shifted on his ass, and made him play *your* game.

WEATHERSPOON: And soon as I said it I knew I had him.

MADDOX: Like with a lady, the first time.

WEATHERSPOON: [*"Right."*] You can *feel* it.

MADDOX: You *know*.

WEATHERSPOON: Wham—[*Holding out his hand for five, as* MADDOX *gives him five.*]

MADDOX: Bam!

WEATHERSPOON: Thank you ma'am.

MADDOX: They don't teach that at Miller High.

WEATHERSPOON: Dox, he did-not-even-blink.

MADDOX: Think maybe you let him off too easy?

WEATHERSPOON: Just kind of nodded, you know, as if to say, "Hell, I was going to burn it down anyway."

MADDOX: So, what you have to do?

WEATHERSPOON: Go to the airport, get a suitcase and tickets from a locker. Take the plane. Switch suitcases with a big heavy ass one in a locker down there, come back home. Put *it* in a locker.

MADDOX: I thought you was going to have to bump off the president or emperor or what ever they got down there. [**WEATHERSPOON** *shakes his head.*]

MADDOX: But you would have done it.

WEATHERSPOON: [*Firing thumb & forefinger "gun."*] Hasta luego, El Presidente.

MADDOX: So?

WEATHERSPOON: So, just that slick, the deed, putting the joint in my name, was here, waiting on me when I got back!

MADDOX: Wham bam. But I still don't know who it was.

WEATHERSPOON: [*"I'm getting to that."*] The very next morning I get back, I'm congratulating myself and having my coffee, it comes on the news: Terrible Tony...

MADDOX: Terrible Tony? You telling me it was *The* Terrible Tony?

WEATHERSPOON: [*"That's who."*] Mmm hmm...

MADDOX: He was the biggest, *baddest*, most notorious...He was to Detroit what Al Capone—one slip with him...

WEATHERSPOON: And Paulette got to cancel a day of shopping to go to my funeral.

MADDOX: Bang, bang, shoot 'em up. I remember when he got killed.

WEATHERSPOON: Found floating under the Belle Isle bridge.

MADDOX: They say so many holes in him looked like granny's lace curtains.

WEATHERSPOON: *That's* what came on the news. It was the morning after I'd made the delivery.

MADDOX: Man. You and Terrible Tony.

WEATHERSPOON: But now all kinds of questions running

through my mind. Who got him? Why? It got anything to do with what I just delivered? What*ever* in the hell that was.

MADDOX: 'Cause if they'll shoot him you can imagine what they'll do to you. And you dealt with him, toe to toe. You took one hellified chance. I'm proud to know you, boy.

★

monologue from
CODA
by Bill Harris

[*Tenor plays as* **MADDOX** & **THERESA** *move to the bandstand, she then begins vamping, as lights go to half on them.*]

WEATHERSPOON: [*Enters. To audience, referring to* **MADDOX** & **THERESA.**] The Detroit way. You know where the word jazz comes from, don't you? From a French word [*With exaggerated French accent.*] *jazzer*. Means to talk, y'know, run it down. Yeah. And you know why I put music in here in the first place? Because I thought we needed it. I mean I got this joint almost like a gift. Ain't every day one of us gets an opportunity like that.

And so, maybe I'll somehow kind of return the favor, y'dig. Make a club of *our own*. Where we can come and hear our music without a whole lot of bullshit from people running it to make a buck, but not respecting the music, or us.

You know I said about Dox cutting Bird: One Friday night it was, and it was a classic. Bird's blowing over at the Rouge Lounge, and everybody who can't get in there is here, figuring he will fall by after anyway. So, it's tight in here as 13 people under a parasol. And right down front, from the opening set; these two chicks. Two of the finest brown skins I have ever seen in my natural life! Drinking Bloody Marys, and wasn't having to pay for a one, courtesy of every dude in eye shot of them. And everybody with a horn is in here in the hopes of getting to blow with Bird when, and if, he shows. But Dox is having none of that; is cutting everybody with nerve enough to unpack his axe.

Now Lilly is on a break, down at the end of the bar, nursing a Coke with just a little ice, same way Theresa takes it, and digging Dox teaching school, and these two chicks digging him. I'm behind the bar trying to help Oscar keep up with the orders.

Okay, so we got Dox, eliminating all competition in anticipation of Bird's arrival; we got these two chicks—You know how when a jungle cat stretches, after a nap, and its muscles like be having a rippling tug-of-war with each other, all slow and sleek and powerful; and how like silk looks sliding across a nipple; and the sound of nylons rubbing together—?—these chicks, when either one-of-them goes strolling to the Ladies during a break! And we got a primed Friday night full-house—And about 2:30 in flies Bird. Excitement runs through the joint like Castor Oil through a cat. Bird immediately digs what's happening, draws his axe and mounts the stage. The pressure cooker is on. The flame is lit!

House rules have always been, new man calls the tune. Bird calls *Cherokee* and takes off like Brer Rabbit through the briar patch! And Dox, Brer Fox, is on him! Like a duck on a June Bug, and is not about to be out run or out done. The crowd is shouting, Blow!

And that's when these two chicks get to clapping their hands, and one of them starts hollering, Go, alto, go! And Bird is digging this chick and is breathing fire and blowing bullets and tearing that little horn up! And when he comes to the end of his solo he quotes, in rapid succession from, "You Came To Me From Out of Nowhere," "I'm In The Mood For Love," and "Now's The Time." Talking to her, y'dig. And right on top of this, almost, Dox comes in with his solo, which he begins by quoting, "All The Things You Are," and, "Things To Come" to this other chick. Then goes into his solo with his ears laid back.

Well the other chick starts hollering, Go, tenor, go! And he does! Chorus after chorus after chorus. Then at the end of his solo he rips off quotes from, "Embraceable You," "You Go to My Head," and "Lady Be Good," aimed at this chick, dig it. Lilly was on her second Coke, light ice, and is just digging all this. Everybody else is screaming. It's so hot in here the walls were sweating and we've almost got to take turns breathing. Now after Dox's solo, him and Bird they start trading 16 bars, then 8, then 4, then 16 again, 8, 4, 2. They wore it and everybody in here *out*. Wasn't a dry nothing in the house. People were screaming, whistling, stomping their feet. It's New Years Eve on benzedrine.

And Bird and Dox are standing there like two fighters, Sugar Ray and LaMotta, after a 15 round war, looking down at Misses Fine and Double Fine.

Lilly finishes her Coke, winks at me, and moves to the stand to reclaim the piano. Now Lilly was known, among other things, for her ability to play long, hard and fast, from her days playing in the churches. She's the new man, right, so she calls the tune. Everybody is expecting another jet, like "Little Willie Leaps," or one of them other race horses. But she goes into a ballad. F'ing everybody up! People are thinking, What's happening, man? Even grumbling a little bit. They want blood. They want to see one of these cats hit this wall doing 900.

But Lilly was cool; like she was sitting in church on Easter Sunday, only thing missing was a little straw hat. Now you know Detroit piano players. They play all of the tune from verse to coda. The Detroit way. And Lilly is all over the piano: Art Tatum and Horowitz. But it was an extremely hip crowd and it wasn't but a minute before they recognize what she's playing: "If I Should Lose You."

Well Bird, leads off, and he's in to it. His little alto kind of resting on his Buddha belly, big sausage fingers—(F'ing drugs had him bloated up) but that don't stop him. Bird's painting pictures. Watercolors, like down in the art museum: like landscapes. With like a little bird with a piece of pretty bow ribbon in its mouth; the blue bird of happiness, gliding through a fluffy-pink-cloud sky. Now it's a whole different thing Bird's painting; people grinning like teenagers at the prom. It's orchard corsages on cotton candy dresses. And Bird steps back, as if to say, now out-pretty that.

And then Dox begins. And it ain't a ballad no more. Lilly is vamping under him and it's like she talking, whispering to Dox and there is nobody else in the joint. A woman talking to her man in that Detroit way like they can do. And it ain't a ballad or even a love song, it's grown folks talking. He's standing there with his back to the audience, blowing directly at her and she is playing and looking directly at him! "If I Should Lose You." And they whispering back and forth.

You might not believe it, but their message was so strong that folks started like easing out two by two, hand in hand. And it wasn't the lateness of the hour that was sending them out of here.

I remember it like it was yesterday. Man, I'd give anything to have a tape recording of that night. My grand kids wouldn't have to work—which would put them in the same category as their daddies.

The two chicks? [*Laughs.*] They both left with Bird. You know—
I never heard either Dox or Lilly play that tune again. Separately
or together. Now they might have, somewhere else, I'm just
saying they never played it in here. [*Light fades on*
WEATHERSPOON, *up on* **MADDOX** & **THERESA** *they play
their duet as lights fade on them and the end of the play.*]

★

monologue from
MAN
by Laurence Holder

A playwright for almost 25 years now, Mr. Holder is noted for evergreen classics such as *When the Chickens Came Home to Roost*. Winner of seven Audelco Awards, the play deals with the final days of the relationship between Malcolm X, dynamic spokesperson for the Nation of Islam, and his surrogate father mentor, the founder and Messenger of the Nation of Islam, Elijah Muhammad, which featured the wonderful late Kirk Kirksey portraying the Messenger and Oscar winner Denzel Washington as Malcolm X. Another classic is *Zora*, about the mystical, mythological novelist and folklorist, Zora Neale Hurston, which originally featured Yvonne Southerland, Phylicia Ayers-Allen, and now Elizabeth Van Dyke. Both were originally produced by Woodie King, Jr., and the New Federal Theatre in 1981. Other critically acclaimed pieces are *Hot Snow*, about the great Jelly Roll Morton, and two contemporary pieces which are excerpted in this volume, *Man*, about a psychopath born and raised in prison; and *Woman*, an abused migrant farm worker who unsuccessfully tries to throw off the cloak of abuse and hatred and murder.

Mr. Holder is a full-time teacher of English at John Jay College and a teacher of poetry and drama at the Dramatic Writing Program of New York University.

Cast: Man
Time: Now
Place: Here

[**MAN** *races onto stage pursued by someone. He hides, peering menacingly and then imploringly.*]

MAN: What the hell do they know? Them cops following me? Why should I be locked up? I didn't do nothing but protect myself. If she comes around to bother me again, I'll do it gain. A woman ought to learn her place. Even a woman from the streets got to know that she's got a place. Well, what do you expect living in Harlem, USA? Heaven?! [*Laughs.*] Jesus! There ain't no Heaven. That's what I was trying to tell that other woman when she put her face in my business. She's got to know even if she's poor like me she can't stick her nose into my business.

What do I give a damn about Jesus Saves? What do I care about that? And then she wants to have a conversation with me. In the supermarket. And I got five steaks stashed in my coat. [*He opens his coat to show his stash.*] I don't have any inclination to talk to her at all. None!

She want to tell me though that they got these meetings at their little church. I knows they got their little meetings at their little church. I seen her and the other old ladies out there trying to get people to get to the church.

But what I want with church! I want to tell her all this bad, but I'm no fool. You know I'm no fool. I keeps my mouth shut and we gradually moving up to the front of the line and then I notice that she ain't got a wagon. She ain't got a basket. All she got is these leaflets and a big mouth. So's I tell her that. "Aint you got food to buy? Why don't you stop messing with me?"

And she had the nerve to say back: "I'm carrying the words of the Lord in my mouth and my heart. And all I want you to do is say that you'll come to the church tonight." TONIGHT! I ain't got time to come tonight. And maybe my voice is a little loud, but you got to excuse that, right? I mean, Jesus, I'm carrying the damned food in my coat. All I'm buying is a little soap, which I hardly use, but it looks good to be buying something and not just walking out looking heavy. Well, the store manager hears me and he knows the woman and he walks on over to us and he starts looking at me strange. I want to punch that woman in the nose in the worst way now, I mean I could get busted and all she wants to know is will I come to the church tonight. Shit! If I'm busted I can't do anything. But she just keeps on talking about how Jesus freed everybody by giving his life on the cross. Now I don't want to hear anymore of this crap because I don't feel free and I know that He was gyped.

And that's when I made my mistake. Maybe I shouldn't have hit her and run. Maybe I shouldn't have hit the manager and run. Maybe I shouldn't have hit either of them and run, but that's all I know in this life. Hit them and run. That's what they been doing to me all my life. Hitting me and running. So I got to do I back to them right? I should have hit them harder, that's what I should've done. Then they couldn't remember who I am. But I know they know who I am, at least what I look like.

Hey! If I got another coat they wouldn't know it was me would they? Of course they wouldn't. How could they? They know a color, that's all. I get a coat with another color and I'm in the clear. That's what I'll do. That's what I'll do. [*Chuckles.*] Now that I fixed up the world's problems I feel better. But the nerve of that woman. And anybody else who thinks that Jesus is the one. Jesus ain't shit. And I'll tell the Pope that. I'd love to tell the Pope that one. I'd love to see the look on his face. His eyes getting strange and his voice choking up and all. Shit, if He was anybody, He'd be driving a big car...and there's lots of big cars out there but I ain't heard or seen of any Jesus. Since Jesus is Black he probably can't get payments. And what does going to heaven mean anyway? This world is too big a place for anybody to keep thinking that they die and go some place where they can live again. Got a lot of fools out there, I just ain't one of them, that's all.

Aint no way I could be a fool, I mean when I was born I didn't have a mother or a father to teach me anything. They were gone. A child of the State Bureaucracy is what they called me. I had a mother—she didn't want me. Who could blame her? What could she do with a kid in jail? Not get a job. She couldn't get out there on the streets and see for anything because she was incarcerated. Like them big words? Thems the ones the social workers taught me. Year after year. Read! I read. Talk! I talked. It got so I could do anything, but everytime they put me on display with a foster parent, even got me into some homes, things never worked out. The folks on the outside were as bad as the ones on the inside. That's what this one social worker said to me any way. He claimed I was neglected and sometimes abused. Interesting word, abused. I mean I was abused by these foster people because they refused to feed me and when I complained, they beat me. But I was used to all that. I was abused by the people in the institutions the same way. They would feed me or not. They would beat me or not. And me being the little person that I am would get beat by the other kids because that's all they knew. Well, shit! If I bother to read a newspaper that's all the governments are doing to each other, beating the shit out of each other anyway they knows how.

Anyway! But I begin to see an angle and so I stand there slackjawed and dumb looking, and let all those social people workers feel sorry for me. Damn right. Feel sorry for me! I ain't got nothing. Ain't never had anything. And the future looks bleak. So feel sorry for me and get me things. And that's what they would do. Feel sorry for me. "Look, your Honor, he was abandoned by his mother in prison. That's right, your Honor, abandoned..."

★

monologue from
WOMAN
by Laurence Holder

Cast: Woman
Time: 1984
Set: Jail cell

[*Lights up on* **WOMAN** *in a jail cell. She is singing "Round Midnight."*]

WOMAN: IT BEGINS TO TELL ROUND MIDNIGHT, ROUND MIDNIGHT...My name is Mattye Robinson. I was born in Gates, Florida, a small town off the Lauderdale expressway. Really small. About the only people living there was my family, mother, father, two brothers, and a tiny sister. Lived in a small shack, had one door to go in and come out. Outhouse in the back. Wasn't many other people around us and when I was a little girl I had a happy time playing, but I didn't have any friends, just my big brothers, and they were always playing football or something. But my mother wouldn't let me play with them. Had very special ways about us. Girls couldn't play with the boys. They could do the same work, but they couldn't play the same way. By the time I was six I was in the fields with the rest of them. We used to pick the tomaties, and the potaties, and the oranges. I used to love being in the fields because when the sun was hot the old folks would slow down and rest awhile, but us young ones would keep on playing until we just dropped. There used to be about twenty families in the fields. We used to pick fruit and the vegetables for the [*Seems to become angry.*] Best Family. John Best was the master, the overseer, the paymaster. And when paydays came all the men of the families would gather around Mr. Best and wait for their money. Always seemed like the Robinson family be getting the last of the change. And my family was the first one in the fields all the time. It never seemed fair. One day all us kids that were about the same age got swept up onto a bus and we went to school.

Now that seemed strange, going to school. I wanted to be out there where the air was, the sun, the clouds, the trees. I sure didn't want to spend a whole lot of time inside staring at some teacher who didn't want to be there teaching us. Could almost see his eyes staring down at us right now, making up his mind that he didn't want to be teaching us, a bunch of screaming six- and seven-year-olds. You see the thing about us, I was beginning to catch on to, was that we was migrants and most of the time the folks didn't even have to pay us in money much less teach us. But there was some new law that people was excited about and that's why we were in school.

I didn't like the law then. And when I got a little older I knew I didn't like the law because it only seemed to protect people like the Bests. Some times when he didn't have enough money to pay us we would have to borrow from him in order to get some money for food. [*Pauses reflectively.*] I never understood that. I once asked my mother was we ever going to get paid for the work we did. I pointed out to her that if you worked you got paid. That's what they were teaching in school. I was already ten or eleven by that time and starting to fill out. My mother looked at me and told me never to make any problems again. What problems! She slapped me and told me that I was to do whatever the white man told me to do. He was the Boss. He was the one who paid. And if he couldn't pay it must mean that he didn't have no money. But that wasn't true. UH HUH! I knew that wasn't true. I had seen Mr. Best spending some big money in the saloon with some of his friends. I told her that and she slapped me again, talking about how I'd better mind my own business and shut up. Two slaps! Not one, but two. I ran out of the house and down the path to my favorite private spot about half a mile off the main dirt road. I went there whenever life with people got too hard for me.

[*Chuckles.*] I must have spent half my young life there. Seemed like people were always crazy, always going off their heads, out their minds, or something. And about the only place I could get peace was there. My face still smarts. Seems like my mother was always hitting me in those days because I was such a smart ass asking questions. But it seems to me that if you got a question you ought to ask it otherwise how you going to find out anything?! And just about everytime I tried to explain that to my mother she'd get a switch or something to make my behind, my life, black and blue. I like to learn how to sing out there but I knew that my brothers would probably hear me and that would be the end of any privacy I had. So I stayed quiet, silent. After awhile. Yeah!

It took me plenty of beatings until I finally got it in my head. And one day, I can remember it real good now, coming real clear to me, something happened and I didn't have to say anything. I didn't want to say anything. I never did.

★

104

monologue from
MOM'S LONG LEASH
by Walter Jones

Walter Jones is a native of Fayetteville, N.C. Mr. Jones has been writing professionally for twenty five years. His plays have been produced at Joe Papp's Public Theatre, (N.Y.C.); Ellen Stewart's Cafe Lamama, (N.Y.C.); Woodie King's New Federal Theatre, (N.Y.C.); Manhattan Theatre Club, (N.Y.C.); The Museum of Modern Art, (N.Y.C.); Smithsonian Institution, (Wash. D.C.), and many colleges and community theatres throughout the Country.

He received a Rockefeller Grant for playwriting, and was a Term writer for Norman Lear and Bud Yorkin's sitcom, *What's Happening.*

[*Sarah goes to her sleeping quarters and turns a blue light on. The lighting should be a blue light shining on Sarah's bed. Sarah picks up telephone and dials while relaxing in bed.*]

SARAH: Hi, Lillian. Girl, where have you been? I've been trying to reach you all week...Nooo you have not been home, I've been trying to get you night and day. Ooooh, so that's what's been happening. A new man in your life? Well, congratulations friend. I hope you all get married and it lasts for a hundred years.

Yes, I really do, because a good man these days is harder to find than a lake in a desert. Oh, I know you've been married twice. A third time isn't going to kill you. In fact, it might be the best thing, now that you have the so-called "marriage experience" behind you. Experience accounts for about everything that you get involved in. Marriage, job, whatever. Noo child...Me husband walked away from me over five years ago. He writes his son a hello note about every two years. Huh? Yes, the return address is usually from a small town in North Carolina. Noo. Why should I let Tommie read them? All he is going to do is get nervous, sad, and start asking questions that I can't answer. I just deposit them in the garbage can. I don't need the hassle. No...Hahahaha girl you stop...hahaha...I don't need nothing. Sex is all in the mind. No child, it has been over two years since any man touched me. You remember the guy I used to go out with, Leon, from my job? Yeap...he sweet talked me, after everything got cozy, he tells me that he is married, but loves me very much but he can't leave his family. Can you believe that? So I told him that I didn't want no other woman's man. I can do without that aggravation I'm not walking around with a sign on, saying "man wanted please call." I keep myself busy...No, I'm not a Jehovah's Witness and I don't belong to a Holy Rolly Church. Sarah girl, you're asking too many pertinent questions. I work five days a week and weekends. I check out grocery at A&P and I take classes two nights a week up at City. My son is not a little boy anymore. He's a thirteen year old teenager. I'm not neglecting anyone, I'm trying to make a better life for myself and my son. THAT IS NOT SOO! That's just a bunch of liars. I know who I am and what I'm doing. Look at you, you're in no position to tell anybody nothing. You're a two time loser with marriage, and you've gone through countless unresolved relationships. You also had an abortion swept under the rug and you're just thirty-two years old. By the time you are thirty-five, you'll be out to pasture with nothing left to give anybody, but your free-spirited mindless lifestyle, BYE! [*She hangs up the phone.*]

★

scene from
THE WITHERING ROSE
by Walter Jones

ROSE: Hey, are you all really hungry? I'll cook up something.

FRANK: We don't want something, we want meatloaf.

ROSE: Now that's all gone.

FRANK: All gone!

ROSE: Yep.

LISA: How can you do that when you knew we were coming?

ROSE: How was I to know that you were coming?

LISA: You should have felt our vibes.

FRANK: I don't want any cake. My stomach calls for some meat and potatoes.

ROSE: I got the potatoes.

LISA: And we can get the meat.

FRANK: What type of meat?

LISA: Meatballs and spaghetti.[**LISA** *looks at Rose.*]

ROSE: Fine with me.

LISA: Frank?

FRANK: Which is the closest store that I can get to and not get mugged?

ROSE: The store across the street is owned by the father of most of the muggers in this neighborhood.

FRANK: His boys made such a profit on mugging, they've put their old man in business?

ROSE: Looks that way.

FRANK: They don't mug their customers?

ROSE: Nope. You'll be safe there.

FRANK: Don't you all miss me too much. I'll be right back.

ROSE: We'll hold our breath til you return.

FRANK: I shall return. [**FRANK** *opens the entrance door and the setting sun, which has reddened, flashes into the room.*]

ROSE: [*Shouts.*] Oooooweeee, close that door, the sun. [**FRANK**

is almost knocked down by the invisible dog.]

FRANK: Doggone dog, watch where you're going.

ROSE: Close the door please.

FRANK: Bye. [*Frank slams the door and rushes to the store.*]

ROSE: Footsie, where have you been for so long? Get on away from here. I don't feel like playing with you now. Teasy, where did you find Frank?

LISA: Where did Frank find me.

ROSE: O.K. Found you.

LISA: At a friend's house who's a cocktail waitress by night and fulltime math student by day. It was a chess party, she's into chess, so I came into the party wearing a beautiful green dress that had a slit down the sides. I was looking as beautiful as I've ever looked in my whole life. I felt like a queen, like the whole place belonged to me. Everybody wanted to dance with me, have a drink with me. Frank, the host, introduced himself to me. We played chess. I beat him three games to two, and then we danced the whole night through. Later, he said my mind interested him more than my body. Although my body isn't too bad at 35 and two offspring. It still is firm and has all the right curves in place.

ROSE: I don't know about that.

LISA: Whether you know about it or not, my body reflects a 35 year old lady who has taken care of it; hasn't over eaten, and I exercise regularly.

ROSE: You're working on catching husband number two?

LISA: I'm not working on catching anyone. You make it sound so bad—working on someone. I enjoyed my first marriage. The first 7 years were absolutely terrific. It really was wonderful, each day exhilarating with the kids and all. Then something happened. Someone pulled a plug, and within a year it all deflated.

ROSE: It always does. Friendship isn't permanent, so why bother.

LISA: Nothing is permanent, not even life. We come here for a moment, then pass right on through. Each day I stride toward a new day. If bitterness comes, I'm prepared for it. For the most part, life has been sweet to me. I look forward to having another good husband.

ROSE: Frank?

LISA: Who knows, who cares. Why all these questions, Rose Sherlock? My goodness, you're worrying yourself to death about Frank and my business. What about your personal life. Huh? How in the world did you allow yourself to get stuck here in a wet and damp basement apartment? Girl, what has happened to you?

ROSE: [*Uneasy.*] Nothing has happened to me.

LISA: Yes it has, child, you're sending yourself down the river. You used to work for the city making good money. The manager of your unit. Accounting and bookkeeping was your thing. You prided yourself on being efficient. You used to brag: "I can type 85wpm and if you catch me on one of my good days, I'll bang out 100 wpm faster than a bat can blink his eyes". I used to enjoy visiting you at the Tracy Towers, in the north section of the Bronx. I'd look out your lovely view from the 17th floor, at the green woodside and the huge mountains in the distance. It was so beautiful. Now you're down here in the south Bronx living in purgatory.

ROSE: [*Shouts.*] Will you shut up! Be quiet! You don't know nothing.

LISA: But how, Rose? How? You're withering away.

ROSE: I'm not withering away. You don't know what you're talking about. I'm not...

LISA: But how?

ROSE: It's not important how or why I did anything. How, how—no, it's only important that I'm here now occupying this space away from a husband who died on me and a lover who did the same and a son who ran away hating me. Away from all the things that have caused me terrible pain. Away from lying co-workers, away—away—away. Now just leave me alone. You're sounding just like my sister. Your visit was enjoyable but now it's becoming boring.

LISA: Alright, alright, but don't let this loneliness get you down.

ROSE: Nothing is getting me down, but you are beginning to get on my nerves.

LISA: Hey, I don't want to do that. Which is the Jane?

ROSE: The what?

LISA: The toilet.

★

scene from
THE COMMITMENT
by Joseph Lizardi

Joseph Lizardi was educated in New York's Public School System and holds degrees from Bronx Community College and Baruch College. He served four years in the United States Marine Corps. His first two plays *The Commitment* and *The Block Party* were produced by Woodie King, Jr. at the Henry Street Playhouse. This was followed by a production of *El Macho* by Miriam Colon's Puerto Rican Traveling Theater.

Mr. Lizardi is the Playwright-in-Residence at the Arena Players Repertory Theater in East Farmingdale, Long Island, where many of his plays have received production, among them *Blue Collars, The Powderroom, December in New York, Three on the Run, Love's Comedy, A John Wayne Kind of Hero*. Mr. Lizardi is a member of the Dramatists Guild.

[*There is a knock on the door.*]

JOEY: [*Crossing to the door.*] Hey, Manny! How you doing, man? Come on in.

MANNY: [*Walking into the living room.*] Can't stay long. I sneaked out of the hospital. [**MANNY** *crosses to the window and looks out cautiously.*] Somebody's following me. [*They look at each other for a long second.*] You look great.

JOEY: Man, when was the last time I saw you? Long time ago.

MANNY: Almost five years.

JOEY: Somebody told me you were living in Puerto Rico.

MANNY: I was. [*Looks out the window.*] When I came back your mother told me you were fighting in Viet Nam. How was it?

JOEY: Man, a bad experience. Two years fighting and I'm back to the same shit.

MANNY: Too bad you didn't get captured.

JOEY: Yeah. How'd you like Puerto Rico?

MANNY: It was all right. I got restless and had to come back. My roots are here.

JOEY: I know what you mean.

MANNY: [*Looks out the window.*] How long have you been home?

JOEY: Eight months. Man, things have really changed around here. From bad to worse. Most of the guys are gone.

MANNY: Pee Wee's still around.

JOEY: Yeh. That's what I've been told.

MANNY: [*His voice is tinged with anger.*] He looked bad the last time I saw him. Remember how we used to call him "The Champ." [JOEY *nods his head sadly. Slight pause. They regard each other for a long second, then* MANNY *looks out the window.*]

JOEY: Hey, man—you still writing poetry?

MANNY: When I'm in the mood. [*Indicating the typewriter.*] You used to write plays—

JOEY: I'm still at it. Hey, can I offer you something?

MANNY: No, man, I don't have the time. Come on, sit down.

JOEY: Man, I haven't seen you in a long time.

MANNY: [*Sitting on the couch.*] Look, I guess by now you know I'm president of the Latin Warriors—

JOEY: I heard about it, but—man, you never went in for violence.

MANNY: Till I did three years in Attica. Armed robbery. Nobody got hurt. It was a cold winter and my father was three months behind in the rent. I did a lot of reading in jail. I went to night school after I came out. [*He rises and looks out the window.*]

JOEY: Look, I heard on the news about the takeover of Jefferson Hospital—

MANNY: That's what I came to talk to you about. That place is a slaughterhouse, full of young doctors eager to cut up people for their own benefit. Man, ninety percent of the patients in that hospital are Puerto Ricans! Fifty percent of them wind up in the morgue!

JOEY: Man, doesn't that happen in every hospital of every ghetto?

MANNY: Sure it does, because nobody does anything about it, man, how would you like to see your mother or your father used as a "guinea pig"?

JOEY: What are you talking about?

MANNY: [*Sitting on the edge of the couch.*] Don Lucas' wife checked into the hospital last week. A simple pain on her side. Within three days she was empty inside. We went to the hospital with Don Lucas. We asked her doctor what was wrong. Man, he just shrugged and said, "More surgery required." But a couple of nights ago she was found dead. [*Rises and crosses to the window as he talks.*] Some of the patients in the ward said she was trying to get to the bathroom. Don Lucas said she was in so much pain she wanted to die. So she lied on that cold floor and bled to death. [*He stands looking out the window, he seems emotionally upset as he takes a few shuddering breaths.*] My mother died in that hospital. Remember her, Joey?

JOEY: Of course I remember her.

MANNY: When I came back from Puerto Rico I brought some

dirt from her hometown and I spread it over her grave. She was a beautiful woman. Man, you ever taken a good look at your mother? And all the others like her? They're tired and weary. Some of them look dead. You know who's their best friend? A God who doesn't give a fuck about them! They only have one dream now—getting $74 together so that they can go back to Puerto Rico and die in peace. Man, they deserve more than that! Last night those prick doctors at the hospital let three Puerto Ricans die because they were junkies. We went in and asked for a medical report and they chased us out. No, man, that machine never works for us. That's what we're going to change and we're starting with that hospital. Show them we can fight back. Man, you want to write a play? Look around you, Joey. You'll find plenty to write about. Now the fuckin' cops are going around turning the people against us. Spreading the word that we're a bunch of radicals and communists tearing buildings down. Nothing but lies. They say nothing about the drug rehabilitation programs we've created—which includes finding out what cops are on the pad. They say nothing about the breakfast programs for hungry kids. Let me tell you, man. Two years ago a kid disappeared from the neighborhood. We looked all over for him. We found him dead in the basement of an abandoned building not far from here. He was eaten alive by a bunch of hungry rats! For two days they were feeding themselves off that poor kid. Man, that would never have happened in Forest Hills or Glendale or Riverdale or Long Island. Why? Because they got political power, and that's what we need. We've got to build our own powerful base so that we can force every politician in this town to worry about our vote. We're lost and confused, Joey. A dying culture. We got no identity. Foreigners with no rights. The shiteaters, back-benders, ignorant peasants. We need you, Joey. We need a spokesman, somebody to write, not to riot and burn, or fight the police. [*Reaches in his pocket and takes out a manila envelope.*] I want you to keep this.

JOEY: [*Taking the envelope.*] What is it?

MANNY: Everything we want to do is in there. We want you to write a manifesto based on it. If you decide to join us, come to the hospital tonight. We'll show you around so you can see for yourself. I gotta split. [**MANNY** *crosses to the door.*]

JOEY: I'll be there.

[*They stand staring at each other for a long second, then they shake hands in the symbolic Latin Warrior's salute.* **MANNY** *goes out and* **JOEY** *stands with his eyes fixed on the closed door. He crosses to the typewriter and sits frowning at it.*]

★

monologue from
THE BLOCK PARTY A Play In Two Acts
by Joseph Lizardi

[**LENA**, *known as a pretty neighborhood prostitute, has just returned from a job interview, angry and frustrated, drinking from a bottle of brandy she keeps in her pocketbook. She meets Don Paco, who owns a nearby bodega, at the stoop of the dilapidated building where she lives with others. He stands listening to her.*]
LENA: Been a long day, Don Paco. Long, hard day. [*She takes out the bottle of brandy.*] Went for a job, you know. A decent job. Secretary. Well, a receptionist. Saw it advertised in *El Diario.* Didn't get it. [*Uncaps the bottle and takes a healthy drink.*] He said I ain't got the right kind of voice. Whatever that bullshit means. Really wanted that job, you know. [*Another drink.*] I practiced every day. "Good morning, Damon enterprises, incorporated." That was the name of the company. "Good morning, Damon Enterprises, Incorporated." Everybody 'round here said I sounded great. Perfect, you know. A whole week practicing. But that asshole at the interview, he said I looked good but sounded terrible. Wanted to spit on his fucking face. But you know what I did? Begged him to try me somewhere else. So he

asked if I could type, so I lied. So he put me in front of this typewriter—and I tried to type. Everybody laughed at me. I was a big fucking joke. [*Another drink.*] I know everybody 'round here laugh when I say I wanna get out of all this shit, but I do, Don Paco. I really do. I don't enjoy what I do. Never did. I hate it. Nothing to be proud, you know. So fucking degrading, you know. I really hate those creepy fucks when they come here looking for me. A few bucks gives 'em the right to own every inch of you. So you just lay there. Let 'em work you over. Anything they want. Anyway they want. Any fucking time they want. [*Another drink.*] Always kept saying "Next creep's gonna be my last one." 'Cause, you know, always had this feeling I could go out there anytime, get a decent job. So today I tried and what happened? Fucking asshole tells me I ain't got the right kind of voice. He made an ass of me, you know. [*Another drink, frowns on the almost empty bottle.*] Wanna know something, Don Paco? I won a beauty contest in High School. I was the prettiest girl in the whole fucking school. For real. And you know what else? I was in love once. Really in love. When I was sixteen. Even made plans to get married. A young boy. My age. Handsome as anything. Real sensitive. Used to play the piano real nice. And he used to write me poems. Many nights, we used to go to his house, and he'd play the piano and recite the poems. Just for me. We loved each other a lot. But then they killed him. The big, bad macho freaks in the town. They hated him 'cause I loved him and not 'em. They used to pick on him, torture him. One night, they made him so ashamed—he didn't know how to swim—but he jumped in this lake, let the filthy waters take the life outta him. They killed him 'cause I loved him. [*Finishes the bottle.*] One night I was praying by his grave, and they came. They hurt me bad, Don Paco. After that, they followed me everywhere I went. Making demands. And I always had to give in to 'em, keep 'em from hurting me. You can't run away from the fuckers. They're everywhere, you know. Waiting to hurt you. [*Suddenly she slams the bottle down.*] But they can never take care of Lena! Oh, I know they think they can. I love when they come here looking for Lena, showing off their big dicks. I love showing 'em they ain't shit. They try, Don Paco. They pay big bucks to try. They wanna see pleasure on my face but all they get's one big fucking laugh. That kills 'em. They hate that, you know. When you make fun of all that macho shit they come wrapped in. They come in big and hard to hurt Lena but they can't. They just make me laugh. [*She fumbles with a pack of cigarettes but can't get one out and throws the pack down angrily.*] That's why I wanted to get that job. To come back here and yell out for all of 'em to hear "FUCK OFF! LENA AIN'T FOR SALE NO MORE! LENA'S FREE AGAIN! AND SHE'S GONNA STAY FREE THE REST OF HER FUCKING LIFE! LISTEN TO ME, YOU MOTHER-FUCKING CREEPS! LENA'S FREE AGAIN!" [*She collapses on the stoop muttering to herself.*] Wanted, you know, hear a new beat, a different parade. Nobody's cheap toy no more. Wanted to tell 'em all, hands off no matter how much. But, the fucks, they won again—[*She springs to her feet, yelling off into the night.*] Yeh! Bring the studs in! Let 'em parade for Lena! I'll show you all you ain't shit! I'll show you it takes more than balls to take care of Lena! Come on! Lena's waiting! Bring on the parade so Lena can die laughing!

[*She laughs hysterically, then collapses on the stoop, shaking and crying.*]

[*Blackout.*]

★

scene from
MUTT AND JEFF, A One Act Play
by Winston Lovett

Mut and Jeff is about two modern-day hobos who venture into
N.Y.C.; the lines are clean, self-explanitory; actors should play the
moment.
SCENE: Lights up on the 42nd Street Hotel room of MUTT and
JEFF. DSL is a table and chair, a trash can; US is a convertible sofa
bed; to the right is a small table with a lamp on it. US of the lamp is a
dresser. Directly behind the bed is a large picture of Teddy
Roosevelt. The only window in the room is to the right of that
picture; DSR is a coat rack with several garments on it.

  As the lights come up, we see JEFF standing at the dresser,
straightening his clothes and combing his hair. He has on a brown
shirt, polka-dot bow tie and black shoes. MUTT is covered in the bed.
His snoring becomes more and more obsessive, until finally he jumps
out of bed and runs about.

MUTT: Come on! Come on! Let's get out of here!!—Before they
catch us. Come on!!

JEFF: Where we going??

MUTT: We got to go—What?—to go. [*Looks around.*]—Where
am I?

JEFF: You're in New York, having one of those nightmares of
yours, them sleep-walking dreams.

MUTT: Ahh, shit!!

JEFF: That must have been your conscience beating you. I've been
calling you for the last half hour.

MUTT: Calling me for what—?

JEFF: To rise and shine. We've got work to do.

MUTT: I'm going back to bed.

JEFF: You must be kidding.

MUTT: No, I'm not. Just watch me. [*He gets in bed.*] Would you mind turning off the lamp?—Do you have to have the lamp on and the shade up too?

JEFF: It's the only way I can get you out of bed. You ought to be thankful I don't have a radio!

MUTT: You do the same thing every morning.

JEFF: That's because you do the same thing every morning.

MUTT: [*He pleads.*] Aw, Jeff!—Give me a few more minutes—pleaassee...

JEFF: Alright. Don't beg me, you know I don't like people who beg! Look, I'm gonna run down to the store and get us a newspaper, so we'll have somewhere to look and find us a job.

MUTT: Right!

JEFF: Which one do you think I should buy?? The *Times* or the *News*??

MUTT: You askin' my opinion???

JEFF: I feel liberal today. Well, which one??

MUTT: The only people who read the *Daily News* are subway riders and electricians.

JEFF: OK, I'll remember that. Now, where's your pants at?

MUTT: On the chair—what a ya want my pants for?

JEFF: Well you know I don't have any money.

MUTT: I only have a quarter—

JEFF: —Don't worry I'll pay you back.

MUTT: You already owe me a quarter.

JEFF: I *said* I'd pay you back!

MUTT: That's the same way you said it in San Antonio.

JEFF: Look, we're partners right?

MUTT: Right.

JEFF: That means we share everything right??

MUTT: Right...

JEFF: Therefore, if you loaned me a quarter I only owe you twelve and a half cents. If you loan me *this* quarter then I'll owe you a quarter. Got it?

MUTT: I never win when you explain things to me, I—never do. Pull the shades down before you go will you?

JEFF: I won't be gone that long. But I'll do it anyway!...La-deeda! [*He goes to window. He has trouble pulling the shade down. Finally it slips out of his hands and "RUNS" atop the window making lots of noise.*]

MUTT: Ah, man, come on—don't do this to me.

JEFF: Would you believe it was a mistake? Really, it was. [*He pulls the shade down.*]

MUTT: Remember—don't go by the front desk.

JEFF: Don't worry, I won't. [**JEFF** *turns off the lamp and exits..* **MUTT** *snuggles in the bed. Lights fade...Music comes up to simulate a passage of time. Pause. Enter* **JEFF**; *he has a newspaper under his arm, turns on lamp. He notices* **MUTT** *still in bed and begins to sing in a loud voice.*]

JEFF: ZIP—A—DEE DO DAA ZIP—A—DEE AY!
MY—O—MY WHAT A WONDERFUL DAY!
PLENTY OF SUNSHINE! HEADIN' MY WAY!
ZIP—A—DEE DO DAA!! ZIP—A—DEE AY!!!

MUTT: [*Sits up in bed.*] It's a sin and a shame what you do to a song.

JEFF: Just as long as you get the picture.

MUTT: [*Getting out of bed.*] I get the picture. My heart ain't in it, but I get the picture.

JEFF: [*Cheerfully.*] It's a little foggy outside but I think everything's going to be alright.

MUTT: That's what they said on the Titanic.

JEFF: No, really, I think everything's going to be just fine. With a little luck here and a little luck there—we might get somewhere today. We might find a job!

MUTT: Yeah, yeah...Did you see the landlord?

JEFF: Nope, and he didn't see me—either. I went out and came back in through the back way.

MUTT: Good.

JEFF: Man, I feel good! There's nothing like New York air to wake up to. Just take a deep breath and feel that—FREEDOM!

MUTT: Where's your slippers at?

JEFF: Ah, over there under the table. [*He continues.*] Just feel that vibration, AHH! humm. [*One slipper is under the table and the other is peeking from under the bed. He gathers both.*]

MUTT: I'm going—

JEFF:—Don't say it...!

MUTT: To the bathroom!

JEFF:—For your morning ritual! Here, you better take the newspaper with you. Be looking in the Want Ads, and hurry up, I have to use it too.

MUTT: Yeah, yeah...[**MUTT** *takes paper, exits right. **JEFF** goes to the chair and sits. After a moment, he stomps his foot on the floor.*]

JEFF: Them damn roaches, trying to take over the room! [*He yells off to* **MUTT.**] And hurry up in there so we can get out of here! [*Looks at his watch.*] It's almost seven o'clock!...Well, can't do nothing until he comes back...See how long he's gonna take...One, two, three, four, five, six, seven, eight, nine, ten—[*The lights begin to fade, but they do not go all the way black, rather they come back up and* **JEFF** *is still counting.*] four hundred ninety-eight, four hundred ninety-nine!—FIVE HUNDRED!! Goddamn, how long are you going to stay in there??!

MUTT: [*O.S.*] Well you know what I'm doing...!

JEFF: You see anything in the Want Ad section?

MUTT: Haven't got that far yet!

JEFF: You've been in there for over five minutes. What are you doing besides number two?? [*We hear a flush of the toilet;* **MUTT** *appears stage right. He speaks meekly.*]

MUTT: OK, you can go in now.

JEFF: Did you leave the window up??

MUTT: No. I forgot.

JEFF: Then let the guy next door go in!

MUTT: [**MUTT** *goes to back wall and bangs.*] OK, buddy, you can go in now! Everything will be alright!!—Just raise the window and everything'll be all right!

JEFF: You'd better start getting dressed so we can leave. [**MUTT** *sits on the bed.*]—You can't get dressed that way!

MUTT: I'm still sleepy.

JEFF: Well, dream about putting your clothes on. Look, I'm already dressed. You think I'm doing it to stay in practice? No, I'm doing it because that's what people do once they get out of bed.

MUTT: You had to get dressed to get the paper.

JEFF: NO I DIDN'T. I could have gone out with no clothes on at all if I wanted to. You know why?—Because this is New York, and you can do anything you want to in New York as long as it doesn't interfere with somebody else's freedom.

MUTT: Well in that case I'm going back to bed.

JEFF: You can't do that! You know we're behind in our rent. The landlord is going to throw us out—any minute now!! You know we have to find work today—or else!—yet you sit there like Humpy Dorie.

MUTT: Humpy-Dorie? I was reading my horoscope in the bathroom and it said today was a day for relaxation and thought.

JEFF: Well that leaves you out on both counts—so why don't you come on and make it easy on yourself—start getting dressed. [**MUTT** *lays on the bed.*]

★

scene from
THE COMMON INTEREST—A One Act Play
by Winston Lovett

CHARACTERS: ANGUS BROWN, a farmer, and JOEY, a 9 year old kid.

SYNOPSIS: The Common Interest is the story of a young boy and a farmer, a father who has been missing for 10 years, and the secret they all have in common. The play takes place on a farm in Iowa in the mid 50s.

SCENE: At rise: we see a farm house. There is grass to either side of it; the back of the house as well as the front porch can be seen by the audience. DSL, in the yard, there is a cut-a-way version of an old broken truck. There are several small gardens near the house. The sounds of chickens and a rooster crowing are heard at certain intervals throughout the play. There are tall blades of grass near the apron of the stage.

In the background, a tall levy can be seen with lots of grass, grazing cows, and two large oval water towers. The farm house is a weather-beaten white. There are 3 old fading bales of hay DSR.

[*As the lights come up,* **ANGUS BROWN** *walks DSL and bends over the apron of the stage. He looks into the tall blades of grass. He is medium height, muscular, has a beard.*]

ANGUS: Come on out here, sonny. [*He motions with his arms.*] Come on now, don't be afraid of me...I ain't gonna hurt you. [**JOEY** *is hiding in the bushes. He slowly moves some of the blades of grass.*] That's right...that's right, come on...[*Strange music comes up.* **ANGUS** *reaches down and grabs* **JOEY'S** *hand, pulls him out of the bushes onto the stage.*] Who you playing this game with? Hide and seek, that's what you playing ain't it? Hide and seek? What's that other game you play when somebody suppose to go and hide and somebody suppose to find 'em? Umm, let's see...

JOEY: [*Meekly.*] You talking about blind man's bluff?

ANGUS: Yeah, that' it. That's the one, blind man's bluff. That what you playing?

JOEY: No sir.

ANGUS: Well what you doing hiding in the bushes?

JOEY: I want to speak with the birds.

ANGUS: Speak with the birds? What for?

JOEY: I figured I could—[*All of a sudden* **ANGUS** *sniffs, frowns, turns his head towards the farm house. We can see smoke coming out of the kitchen windows.*]

ANGUS: HOLY SMOKE! I left my black-eye peas on the stove!! Come on!! [**ANGUS** *runs into the farm house, jumping over rows of Garden foods, his overalls flopping every way they please. He darts through the back door.*] OUCH! OUCH! Goddamit!!—Aw, shucks!! [**JOEY** *slowly walks to the back door and sits on the steps, hands on cheeks. Momentarily* **ANGUS** *appears and stands over* **JOEY**.] I knew I shouldn't have put those peas on!—Now I got to clean that whole pot again. One more second and the whole house would have been on fire. [**JOEY** *looks up.*] You see what you made me do? Come looking for you and I almost burnt my food! And my house. Do you think you're worth all that? [**JOEY** *resumes hands on cheek position.*] Move over and let me sit side you...[**ANGUS** *closes the screen door and clumps down beside* **JOEY**.] You know this is the second time today that you've run off. I'm not going to come after you again. [**JOEY** *looks at* **ANGUS**.] I was lucky to find you this time. If your Aunt Delphine didn't think it was right, she never would have let you come stay with me, right?...Now I realize we ain't had proper time to get acquainted, I mean but I'm willing. Now, if you'll just give me a chance, we can be friends.

JOEY: I won't run away anymore. [**ANGUS** *jumps up and down all over the chicken yard.*]

ANGUS:—AHHH, OW-WEE! [*Sounds of chickens fluttering and making noises can be heard.* **ANGUS** *hugs* **JOEY** *too tightly;* **JOEY** *frowns.*] Oh, my God! I'm sorry...I didn't mean to hug you too tight. You alright?...Whew. It's just that—well—man—I never thought I'd get you to talk. And after this morning when you run off, I mean, I never expected to find you, and I was trying to figure out what to tell Frank. You know he was gonna kill me if you ain't here when he comes. And, well, boy—[ANGUS *starts to hug* JOEY *again.*]

JOEY: No, no!—Don't hug me again!!

ANGUS: OK, OK, if you say so. Come on in the house and I'll fix you a jelly sandwich and some milk. How 'bout that? [*They both stand up.*]

ANGUS: —Wait. Give me your word you won't try to run away again. Give it to me.

JOEY: I promie...[*Clears his throat.*] I promise. I promise.

ANGUS: Shake...Alright, after you, sir.

[*Lights fade on the back of the house and rise on the kitchen. There is a table and chairs, cabinets against the walls with overhead cupboards. The kitchen is the first room from the back porch.* ANGUS *goes to the refrigerator and brings out jelly and milk as* JOEY *sits at the table.*]

ANGUS: [*Fixing sandwich.*] Yeah, make yourself comfortable, you ought to be hungry anyway. Everything is alright now 'cause we're gonna be friends. Yeah...hear that sound coming from outside?...look out that window there...[*The strange music comes up again.*]...That whistling sound is the one I'm talking about. You hear it?? [JOEY doesn't hear anything. The music fades out; ANGUS continues.] Sounds are always right, they're never wrong. That's the sound which means everything is alright. [JOEY *tries again to listen for the sound.* ANGUS *interrupts.*] Do you like your jelly spread thick or thin? Say, boy, I'm talkin' to you.

JOEY: I like mine thick with peanut butter.

ANGUS: But I ain't got no peanut butter. You want it thick or thin?

JOEY: Medium.

ANGUS: "Medium?" What's a medium jelly samich?—That's a joke, son, ha-ha-ha! Laugh.

JOEY: Oh, ha-ha-ha!

[**ANGUS** *gives* **JOEY** *the sandwich.*]

ANGUS: Here. This ought to keep you quiet for a while. Now—sit down at the table before you spill it. [**JOEY** *goes back to chair, but spills some jelly on the floor.*]

JOEY: Oops. That's my fault.

ANGUS: No it ain't—I forgot to cut it in half...[**ANGUS** *places a saucer on the table and a tall glass of milk.* **JOEY** *silently eats. We can see he enjoys the sandwich and the cold milk.*] I got to go outside for a minute. It's time to feed the chickens. You just relax, be right back.
[**ANGUS** *goes out the back door, picks up a pail, goes OSR. We hear him off stage.*] [*O.S.*] "Here chickie, chickie, chickie..." [*We hear the chickens steadily plucking the grain off the ground.* **JOEY** *finishes his sandwich just as* **ANGUS** *comes back through the door.*] Now that's what I call timing. That's the way you and I are going to work around here. 'Cause everything depends on timing. If you can't do things on time—you might as well forget it.

JOEY: Yes sir.

ANGUS:—GOOD, AIN'T IT??

JOEY: What?

ANGUS: The jelly samich. Ain't it good??

JOEY: Yes, sir. It was delicious.

ANGUS: And you can stop calling me "sir". Since we gonna be friends you can...can just call me Angus. [JOEY *shakes his head "Yes." At that moment the sound of an airplane flying low is heard. The sound grows until the airplane passes over the house causing a bottle of ketchup to fall from one of the shelves.*] AW SHIT! Tell me why? Evr—everytime one of them airplanes go buzzing by the whole damn house go to shaking and rattling. [*He gets up from table, goes to back porch, returns with mop.*] Just because we out here in the country—they think they can fly so low. I bet they don't do that in the city.

JOEY: Mr. Angus where is my Daddy? [ANGUS *stares, surprised at the question.*]

ANGUS: What did your Aunt Delphine say?

JOEY: She said—that he was on a long trip—and he was coming home soon.

ANGUS: Well there's no need for me to tell you anything else. All she asked me to do was let you stay here a few days until he came for you. [*Enter SALESMAN, dressed in a suit, carrying a case.*]

★

128

scene from
RUMSHUMKRUSHAFU A Full-Length Play With Music
by Malík

_____

Residing in Jamaica, New York, Malík is a playwright, free-
lance writer and poet. Part of Studio Works for Dianne McIntyre's
Sounds In Motion Dance Company, *RumShumCrushAfu* won a 1988
Christina Crawford Award or playwriting. Other work includes *Get
The One With The Star On The Side*, produced by the Afro-American
Repertory Company and Columbus Stage in Ohio *The Murder of
Cyrene Vignette*, produced by the Frank Silvera Writers' Workshop;
and *Story of a Tree*, currently touring New York City Public Schools
under the auspices of Don Quixote Experimental Children's Theatre.
Publications include *The American Theatre, African Commentary* and
Players magazines. His poetry appears regularly in *Big Red News* and
is anthologized in *Many Voices, Many Lands* and *Paths Less Traveled*.
With his wife,Vassie, he has performed his poetry at, among other
places, Nuyorican Poet's Cafe, Wetlands, the Countee Cullen Library
and Riverside Church. He is a contributing writer with Outta
Control, a multi-ethnic comedy troupe based in New York. Malík is
vice president of Adamfo Kuw (Friendship Society), a cultural
organization which, among its other activities, conducts tours to West
Africa. Jai Guru Dev.

Author's Statement: *RumShumKrushAfu* is a full-length, ensemble
piece using ritual, dance, movement, music from the African and
African-derivative cultures. Hence, the silent images evoked by these
facets of the culture are as important to the movement of the piece as
are the words..

Originally entitled *The Obelisk, RumShumKrushAfu* is a two
character ritualistic/expressionistic drama. It was first read at the
Frank Silvera Writers' Workshop in 1981. Subsequent
developmental readings took place at the Workshop in 1986 and
1988. Play was also read at the Philadelphia Play Works Company in
1989. Additionally, *RumShumKrushAfu* received a staged reading as
part of the Studio Works at Dianne McIntyre's Sounds In Motion
Dance Studio and is a recipient of a 1988 Christina Crawford Award.
It is the first in a trilogy of works exploring the common dilemma of
Africans in the diaspora.

SYNOPSIS: In the scene below, CANDYMAN has stumbled into a
hut from which he will never leave. The reality is that he is a soldier
recently killed in battle. The hut is Purgatory—or middle passage to

the other side, Rumshumkrushafu. NEFI is his spirit guide. He is rife with denial, not only of his own death: but of his Africaness as well. Taunting him with truths and her experience from the other side, NEFI tries to reel him in from those denials. But, she struggles with her attraction for him and his more recent experience with the physical world.

CHARACTERS:
NEFIA—young woman of color, lithe, dreadlocks, mysterious, mystical.
CANDYMAN—An American soldier of color, young, mercenary.

SCENE: The fictional island of Jahlapa. Suspended in mid-air, in the center of the stage, is the thatched roof of a hut, a dome of sorts, sitting over an obelisk. This structure is composed mainly of the human wreckage of war and Egyptian hieroglyphics.

TIME: Now and tomorrow.

[CANDYMAN *sits in one corner of the hut fiddling with his dysfunctional radio—occasionally, it crackles.* NEFI *sits in the other corner of the hut, rocking back and forth.*]

NEFI: Ya got a gal to miss ya in yar Offland?

CANDYMAN: In Worcester? [*A beat.*] Yeah! Yeah! Got me plenty of females back home. Onliest thing is, I ain't ready to settle down. They all be sendin' me letters and shit, talkin' 'bout how much they loves the Candyman. I be tellin' all of 'em to do what come natural, 'cause the Candyman is sure gonna be doin' likewise and otherwise. Just read they letters and laugh. Then I rolls my get-high up in the paper. Can't get good rollin' papers down below...

NEFI: Hark 'e. The fluttering of a locust's wings...

CANDYMAN: Something wrong?

NEFI: Ya got looks liken to he, but yar word ain't crack he trut'!

CANDYMAN: You heard somethin', then? [*He gets his rifle and goes to door of hut.*]

NEFI: No'ting. [*He sets rifle aside; goes to his pack and rolls a "joint"; goes back to door.* **NEFI** *begins to hum "Oh Freedom".*]

CANDYMAN: So quiet out there. Sun'll be up soon. Mist rollin' in over the city. Can't even see the lights down there. The guys hate it when it's like this. Can't distinguish Freedom Fighters from Bystanders, till they up on you and your gonads is hangin for trophies in some Freedom Fighter's hut. [*He lights "joint."*] Never know a war was goin' on the way they be singin' in the Bystander camp. Singin' that old homey shit. Keeps us awake all night, sometimes...[**NEFI** *stops singing.*] Stopped now. Maybe that's what you heard.

NEFI: Heard no'ting, I.

CANDYMAN: Goddamn! How you stand it up here all by yourself?

NEFI: Never by meself. But always alone, I. [**CANDYMAN** *glances sharply at her.*] Got me mudda for comfort...

CANDYMAN: Oh, I get it...[*He laughs loudly.*] You talkin' 'bout that hebejebe mess...

NEFI: Yar mudda give ya comfort?

CANDYMAN: Ain't got no mother. [*A beat.*] Hey, listen? Why was you astin' me 'bout my females back home?

NEFI: Don't recall, I.

CANDYMAN: Maybe you was thinkin' 'bout the Candyman in that way, huh?

NEFI: Was just trying to make conversation.

CANDYMAN: [*He moves towards her.*] You kinda cute for a darkskinned female.

NEFI: [*Moves away.*] Me mudda was dark an' uncommonly pretty, wit' daggers for she eyes an' fire for she words...till ya Offlanders made she cut she locks an' sell 'um one by one for she food...[*Begins to move enticingly.*] Ya won't make Nefi cut she locks, will ya, Zombie? I would die of shame, like me mudda...[**CANDYMAN** *searches his pack for money.*]

CANDYMAN: [*Inattentive.*] Why'd I make you do that?

NEFI: An' ya don't t'ink me hips too big? [**CANDYMAN** *holds up money.*] Don't matter. Gotta make a profit. That's all that counts. Might could even get yourself a little set-up down in the city.

NEFI: [*Trance like.*] An' ya look so han'some in yar zombie greens...

CANDYMAN: Whadaya say? Female down below only costs fifty billion. Jalopey money. And her family'll throw in a goat and coupla hectares of land to boot—

NEFI: Ya smell so sweet, liken to we Jahlapa eart' before ya zombies trample she...

CANDYMAN: Just this cologne I bought on the market down below...

NEFI: Eyes liken to fine crystal...[*Speaks in another voice.*] Eyes that wander! Memories held aloft to neon suns! Forgotten! Cold! Turned inside-out! [**CANDYMAN** *moves back.* **NEFI** *speaks in her own voice again.*] Ya can't take Nefi away from here!

CANDYMAN: Don't wanna take you nowhere!

NEFI: Ya wan' take me to yar Offland. Yar land of the locusts. Nefi can't accept yar proposal of marriage...

CANDYMAN: Look, lady, ain't nothin' but a roll and a tumble! [*He puts his money way.*]

NEFI: Maybe, too, yar buddies got lost in we hills.

CANDYMAN: I ain't lost!!! Just got detached from my unit, is all!!! And my buddies can take care of theyselves!!!

NEFI: Ya zombies always getting—

CANDYMAN: Stop callin' me that! I ain't no zombie! Might could find out just how much of a zombie I am, if you hadn't ruint it for me! Shit! Friggin' females is all alike! Get a guy stahted and...[*Mimics a woman' s voice.*] No...no...no...[*He sits against the obelisk. NEFI reacts violently.*]

NEFI: Move quick, zombie!

CANDYMAN: [*Jumping up.*] You hear freedom fighters on the move?

NEFI: Ya'd smell 'um first. Like I smelled ya. All gussied up in yar fancy parfume from down below.

CANDYMAN: They out there! I know they are! [*Grabs her; pushes her toward door of hut; listens.*] Well, what they waitin' for?

NEFI: Ya got healed from yar disease?

CANDYMAN: Ain't got no disease?

NEFI: One ya got from yar concubine gals in yar Offland? Disease that makes ya burn up their love letters? [*A sound off stage.*]

CANDYMAN: You heard that?

NEFI: Could be ya heard me mudda's song wafting across we barren hills...[*Sings.*]
　　　　"Nkosi sikelel i Afrika
　　　　Malupakam upondolwayo
　　　　Yiva imitandazo yetu..."
Hear it all the time, I, on nights like tonight. When we gentle breezes turn angry an' cold, she song warms Nefi...

CANDYMAN: Stop tryin' to spook me!!! That wasn't no breeze I heard! It was like...like this baby useta cry down the alley back home. My window was right on the alley. This baby useta cry all night and all day long, for the longest kinda time. You could block out most everything else you heard—folks fightin', gunshots—but you couldn't blook out this baby's cryin'. It was like somethin' was wrong—like somebody had left it untended to. One day I ast my old man about it. He got up from his chair, came over to me— lookin' me dead in the eye all the time—and slammed me in the gut. Doubled me over. Was like a rock had hit me. It was the onliest time he ever hit me. Didn't say nothin'. Just ran out of the house. Baby stopped cryin' after awhile. And I couldn't sleep for a whole week after, wonderin' what happened...

NEFI: Ya hear no babies cryin' here. Bystanders say we gentle breezes are gone forever. Gone to Rumshumkrushafu, where no man, no woman, no want no'ting. Once dreamt of going there, I, to meet the keeper...

CANDYMAN: Sun's gotta come up! Just ain't natural. Must be a heavy cloud cover. Look, we got a better chance out in the open...

NEFI: Was legendary, he...

CANDYMAN: Once we get back down to the city, you can stay in one of them Bystander camps set up near base...

NEFI: Could rip the wings from the locust, he...

CANDYMAN: Camp got all the modern conveniences in it...

NEFI: Till they t'ief he trut' an' rip treasure from he heart...

CANDYMAN: Won't let nobody hurt you...

NEFI: Was the only man Nefi ever wanted...

CANDYMAN: You just shut the hell up, now!!! [*He picks up his rifle and his pack.*] All right ! Move out ! [*End Scene.*]

134

Monologue from
RUMSHUMKRUSHAFU
by Malík

This monologue happens after CANDYMAN has tried
unsuccessfully to escape the hut and is bitten by a snake. He speaks
on the pain of being a young man of African descent, and,
simultaneously, the pain of denial of his Africaness. His confrontation
with "the Nazarene" is not so much a confrontation with a better
basketball player. It is a confrontation with his own system of self-
effacing beliefs about his own culture.

[**CANDYMAN** *sits in a corner of the hut nursing a wound.*]

Got enough problems bein' what I am! Before they shipped us
over here, I sent the commander-in-chief a letter, sayin' how I
would like to be sent somewhere where I could finish learnin' my
trade. This sergeant opens it and laughs, sayin' a good fightin'
man is priceless and that I got the best credentials and experience
he seen on a fightin' man in all his days in the pacification forces.
[*A beat.*] Okay. Yeah. Once I did dream of bein' a ball player. You
know, shoot some hoop. That's all I wanted to be. Sometimes it
was more'n a dream. I ate, slept, shat and drank ball. Was good,
too. Was like sweets in a diabetic's pocket when I threw up the
ball. Outside. From the key. In traffic. Like sweets. Came to be the
Candyman to everybody on the court. And soon, guys in the 'hood
stahted callin' me that. Called me it so much till I wouldn't answer
to no other name. Far as I was concerned, I didn't have no other
name, and couldn't remember a time when I was anything but the
Candyman...[*Goes to door of hut, listens for a moment.*] Then, this
new guy move to the 'hood. Dufus lookin' somma'sucka. Black
like coal. First time he hits the court, I knew...like...it was...I was
dog meat. He was all over me. I couldn't hit one shot. Fast break?
He was already at the other end of the court, his hand on the back
board, waitin' to block my shot. Guys stahted callin' him the
Nazarene, 'cause of the way he always landed after a shot—like
he was hangin' from a cross...[*A beat.*] Me? I couldn't get in the
game most times, 'count of him. Lost interest. And then this
somma'sucka disappears. Just like that. Stays around just long

enough to snatch my piece of the dream, then gone! Poof! Some
folks say he got killed in a shoot out with the cops up in Boston.
Him and some other dudes call theyselves schemin' to change
things. I ain't picked up a ball since. They play ball on base, but I
stay to myself mostly...

[*End.*]

★

monologue from
DENMARK VESEY
by Clifford Mason

SCENE: VESEY is on trial as an escaped slave and possible terrorist.

VESEY: What're you waiting for, a full house? You want to
really make the spectacle a big one, do you. What's the quota? At
least a dozen heads. Will there be a full dress parade with the
drum and bugle corps playing the national anthem? Will you force
little Black children to watch so they'll always remember what
happens to bad niggers and grow up to be nothing but good ones?
Is that how you're going to set an example? You're masters at the
greatest trick of a civilized race. How to make savagery and rape
and cruelty respectable. Everything here is according to the law.
As long as you have a law to hide behind, you'll use it to destroy
the minds and bodies of an entire race of people. And it's all legal.
And when the time comes that you can't use that law any longer,
you'll throw it away and get a new one. You might change the
sound and the look and the words, but it will still be the same old
thing. And we'll be the ones that will have to pay the price for
your barbarity. But when on this God's earth will you do the right
thing because it is the right thing and not because the wrong thing
doesn't work any more. You've blasphemed against God and his
holy word. You've used the bible and the law of man and nature to
commit genocide. "Servants, be obedient to your masters..."
Indeed. "All men are created equal..." Indeed. Missouri
compromise indeed. But I'm not a man and the others, they're not
men...I don't have to admit to anything. There shouldn't even be a

trial, because there shouldn't even be such a thing as human slavery. The logic for it doesn't exist, not in this country. Especially not in this country. By every act and episode of your own history, you, above all men, should be the defenders, to the death, of man's liberty. If this were an English court and I stood condemned by the Crown, that would have a logic, just though it would be, it would lie within the realm of British history as a fact to be faced and to be dealt with, to be expected. But not the sons and daughters of the Revolution. Not the children of the men who died at Valley Forge, not the country whose most precious holiday, the Fourth of July, which is just two days away, is a celebration of freedom from tyranny! Give me liberty or give me death INDEED! [*He sits.*] Defense rests.

★

scene from
DENMARK VESEY
by Clifford Mason

SCENE: BUTCHER has just given testimony that has obviously condemned VESEY and a number of others. BUTCHER has been testifying anonymously and VESSY has asked that his identity be revealed, suing for the right to face his accuser.
He has won that point and the judge orders BUTCHER's hood removed. He stands revealed as VESEY cross-examines.

VESEY: Well, hello, Butcher. Butcher Gibbs. [**BUTCHER** *doesn't answer.*] What did they promise you, Butcher, your freedom? Did you sell your freedom for the lives of, God knows how many men? Men who never did you any harm for as long as you knew then? Or are they just gonna give you a chaw of tobacco and a mule and let you set in the shade for a spell? Ole Butcher, yes, sah. Afraid to show your face, huh? How you gonna feel when you walk down the street and see the faces of the people who've trusted you all your life. You gonna be able to look 'em in the eye? Course you will, 'cause they won't know will they? Only those nice folks up there and you will know. And maybe me, if I'm alive....Now, Butcher, let's get down to the business of your testimony. Let's begin with this Africa business. [*He's close to him now.*] You say that I told you that we were going to get help. [*He waits.*]

BUTCHER: [*Looks at his lawyer, who nods. Then, as if clever.*] Repeat the question.

VESEY: Repeat the question. Now if that don't beat all. Repete the question. Why you done turned into a lawyer on me, Butcher.

BUTCHER: No need to be talkin' to me like I'm ignernt. You can talk to me high tone, just like you talk to them. Hmph.

VESEY: Sho nuff. I do declare, Butcher, you are a card. Yes, sir. The ace of spades. That's what you are, Butcher, the absolute, living ace of spades...Now I asked you plain once. This time I'll ask you fancy. Specifically, in what manner was the hypothetical aid from Africa to be taken advantage of?

BUTCHER: I don't know what you're talkin' about.

VESEY: Now, Butcher, you ain't no fool, are you? You mean to tell me you just took my word for it. I mean, didn't you have any questions about it?

BUTCHER: No. Whay should I?

VESEY: Well, was it East Africa or West?

BUTCHER: I told you, I don't know.

VESEY: But, Butcher, how did I communicate with them? By roots, or pigeons, or drums? Do you think that if I stood on Bay Street, right down by the warf and played a drum as loud as I could that they'd be able to hear it in Africa?

BUTCHER: I don't know.

VESEY: Awright, Butcher, what about Haiti? Could they hear it in Haiti?

BUTCHER: Don't know.

VESEY: Is Haiti farther away than Africa?

BUTCHER: [*As if clever.*] Farther away from what?

VESEY: Oh, you're clever, Butcher, I swear. Farther away from South Carolina.

BUTCHER: 'Course not.

VESEY: How do you know?

BUTCHER: 'Cause nothing's farther away than Africa. [*As if clever.*]

VESEY: You don't know how right you are. Now, how was this help gonna come? By boat?

BUTCHER: Of course.

VESEY: And where and when were they going to arrive? And, how many were there?

BUTCHER: Don't know.

VESEY: The question is, whose plans were they? Mr. Butcher Gibbs' or mine. Now, you said there were six thousand men. Six thousand! Whoa, now that's a whole lot a men. How many of 'em did you see?

BUTCHER: Not many.

VESEY: Well, if you was so much in the know, how come?

BUTCHER: 'Cause you didn't want me to know too much in case I got caught. You just told me enough to get me interested, that's all.

VESEY: Well, just how many did you see? A hundred?

BUTCHER: No.

VESEY: Fifty?

BUTCHER: No.

VESEY: How many, Butcher?

BUTCHER: Ten, maybe fifteen.

VESEY: Fifteen men to take over the city with another six thousand from where you don't know. And with help from Africa or Haiti, whichever one is farther away. I swear Butcher, you tell a tall, tall tale. Now, you stated that I told you that Congress had already made the Blacks free, but that the White people in South Carolina wouldn't do it.

BUTCHER: That's what I said.

VESEY: Well, now how did I find this out?

BUTCHER: You read it.

VESEY: Oh, I see. Where'd I read it.

BUTCHER: Somewhere, I don't know.

VESEY: The Missouri Compromise, maybe?

BUTCHER: Yeah, that's where, the Missouri Compromise.

VESEY: [*Shakes his head.*] I read it in the Missouri Compromise. I swear. You know, Butcher, accordin' to you, if I told you that dog shit was money, you'd try to go out here and spend it.

★

scene from
MA ROSE
by Cassandra Medley

Cassandra Medley is from Detroit, Michigan. Her one-act monologue, *Ms. Mae*, is one of several individual sketches which comprise the Off-Broadway musical, *A...My Name is Alice*.

Her one-act play, *Ma Rose*, was produced in The Ensemble Studio Theatre Marathon (1986). The following year, her one-act monologue, *Waking Women*, was produced in the Ensemble Studio Theatre Marathon (1987). After receiving a commission from the Women's Project and Productions to extend *Ma Rose* into a full-length play, it was then produced by that company in October of 1988. *Ma Rose* was also produced by the Eureka Theatre of San Francisco in April of 1990. *Ma Rose* is published by Applause Books in the anthology, *Womenswork* (1989), edited by Julia Miles. Most recently she has had short plays published in *Binnewater Tides*.

Cassandra is the 1986 recipient of the New York Foundation for the Arts Grant, and a New York State Council on the Arts Grant for 1987. She was a 1989 finalist for the Susan Smith Blackburn Award in playwrighting and won the 1990 National Endowment for the Arts Grant in Playwriting.

She is an artist fellow of the Albee Foundation, The Blue Mountain Center, The MacDowell Colony and Yaddo.

CHARACTERS:
MA ROSE—An elderly black woman in her 90's.
VERA ROSE—Ma Rose's daughter, a light-skinned black woman, 55-60.
ROSA—Vera's daughter, dark-skinned, mid-30's, very fashionable business woman.
WAYMAN—Ma Rose's son, 65.
ETHEL—Wayman's wife, 55-60.

SETTING: A small midwestern town, various scenes
interchange between Ma Rose's house and Wayman's house. Act 2, Scene 1 takes place in the church basement of a city, 200 miles from Ma Rose's small town.

TIME: Early December, 1980.

The play moves back and forth in Rosa's memory. The set should have a warm quality and yet be sparse with minimal pieces suggesting the over-all effect of sound and lighting.

SCENE: Spotlight up on ROSA. She sits on the edge of a bed, dressed in a white, silk kimono. Lights come up on a separate area of the stage and we are back in the past in ROSA's mind. There is the sound of gulls and other birdcalls, and the languid lapping of waves.

[MA ROSE *appears, dressed in a casual house dress and barefoot. She is a younger woman again. She is clapping and laughing.*]

MA ROSE: [*Motioning to* VERA.] Come on, Vee—Let's wade on in—let's try it!

VERA: [*Laughing and removing her shoes,* VERA *enters. She mimes approaching the shoreline of a large body of water.*] Momma, you are something else! Ha! Look at you Lord—and she don't even have a swimming suit! Out here stripping—lookit Miss Sexy—[*Laughing.*] Momma, you are a mess.

MA ROSE: I wanna wade on in—

VERA: But it looks deep—Why, I don't even know if Negroes are permitted over on this side—You are something Momma!

MA ROSE: [*Warmly holding* VERA's *cheek.*] You trust me. Just hold onto me.

VERA: [*Also gesturing to* ROSA.] Lil Ro? Come on! Let's see if Momma can hold you—

MA ROSE: [*Also gesturing to* ROSA.] Come on, Baby—Just hold onto Momma and hold on to me.

ROSA: [*Staring out with a tentative but very hopeful smile on her face.*] That's right! Hold me—hold me tight—hold on to me. [*Lights down on the memory.* VERA *silently appears at* ROSA's *side,* ROSA *startles.*]

VERA: [*Quizical to* **ROSA.**] Huh? [**ROSA** *lets out a forced "laugh" and shakes her head, "nothing".* **ROSA** *has walked to the front of the stage and appears to be gazing out of a window. There is the sound of a fierce wind blowing outdoors. Both women gaze out.*]

VERA: Ha' mercy and if we hadn't showed up today—Momma could be right now standing out there in the storm—out of her head and snow piling up around her! [**ROSA** *and* **VERA** *cross over to a simple low platform center stage which suggests a bed surrounded by darkness and void.*]

VERA: Look what I turned up! My "Mz. Sassy"! My Mz. Sassy! Ha. [*Pause.*] [*She holds up the doll.*] Used to give her spankings and whippings and more spankings and ohhh ha! Lord lookit this—lookit what I done come up with!

ROSA: Used to give her "whippings" did you?

VERA: Ha. Oh, yes-s-s-s...used to hide up here underneath the bed here...see...after one of my whippings? [*Hiding up the doll.*] And I'd crawl up under here and—[*She stops abruptly.*] Oh, I don't remember. [*She fingers* **ROSA**'s *kimono.*] Silk. Pure silk.

ROSA: It's a kimono, Mom.

VERA: Yeah, but your bosom half-shows when you raise your arms, so what's the sense of it? That's what y'all sophisticated ladies wear in New York?

ROSA: Am I just chilled? Is that what—'Cause I can't stop shaking—I just oou—I just—I just.

VERA: Now-now—never mind now—Come on here you take one half—I'll take one half. [**VERA** *indicates the blanket and* **ROSA** *crawls in beside her.*]

VERA: Ooou, girl, don't you be touching me with them icicle-toes!—Don't touch me! You stay on your side now—go on!

ROSA: [*Laughing.*] Hey, but you snatching all the cover, Ma— See there, now you tell me "come on in" then you bunch it all up to your side—

VERA: You gonna hafta get out anyway soon 'cause I'm gonna be sleep. You gonna hafta get on back out in the cold...

ROSA: [*Opening the Bible.*] Okay, Mz. Vera-Rose...What verse you wanna go to sleep to?

VERA: Ah, ain't you sweet. Read me something from the Psalms, please, Ro.

ROSA: "Psalms" [*A beat.*] Love the feel of that going through my throat..."Psalms" ...[*A beat.*] Can't stop shaking, Mom.

VERA: [*She spreads her hands over the quilt.*] Hey, Ro, I recognize this! This here's a piece of Great Grandma's head rags here, so you know this must be near a century old...and here's a piece of my Daddy's long john...Just think, your Ma Rose brought 10 living babies into birth laying up underneath this here—There be many lives bound up with a old piece of tatter!

ROSA: [*She smoothes her hands over the quilt.*] Your Daddy—

VERA: Your Grandad—wish you'd known him.

ROSA: What about my Daddy, Ma—

VERA: Now, that's one thing 'bout Ma Rose, boy!! Boy, did she stand up for me!

ROSA: She seems to have liked Daddy.

VERA: 'Cause his people, them Negroes was the worst buch of "pure-blood" thinking so and so's you ever wanna meet—his Momma come chiming I was "too yella tainted" for her precious boy—! Boy, you shoulda seen Ma Rose light into that woman! And in full view of the wedding guest, too—[*She pauses.*]

ROSA: Tell me—was he—? Tell me something 'bout him—

VERA: [*Looking* ROSA *over.*] Pure silk you say? Oh, if Eli coulda lived to see you—just to think—me a 15-month bride laying 'cross that coffin with my dress soaked in breast milk and trying to figure rhyme or reason for this world and what in the world did God intend for me to do—[ROSA *suddenly places each hand on top of* VERA*'s for a beat.*]

ROSA: But what was he like—? [*A beat.* VERA *is clearly in too much pain to open the subject.*

VERA: [*Speaking to herself in a revelry.*] Ha—had me at least something she couldn't snatch from me—something for me to have to myself at last—till Jesus decided he needed him—

ROSA: [*She leans into* VERA *eagerly.*] "She"? Ma Rose? "Snatch from you"—who—who snatch from you—who?

VERA: Hush, that ain't nothing—Christ say "Let the dead bury the dead."

ROSA: [*Eagerly piecing things together.*] You mean Ma Rose. Tell me, woman-to-woman, tell me.

VERA: [*Abruptly reaching for the Bible.*] We gonna find us some Peace of Mind in this here and then get to bed and call it a night and get rest, that's what—[*Finding a passage.*] Here, now lemme hear that "pleasing" voice—sound it out—

ROSA: [*She stares at* VERA *in frustration, pauses, then reads in a dull voice.*] [*Reading.*] "I cried unto God with my voice and he gave ear unto me..."

VERA: Gotta tell ya—sound like you come to them words like a stranger passing through some unfamiliar place.

ROSA: It's time you got to know me—wanna be up front with you—first thing is, I guess you know by now I'm not too religious.

VERA: Ain't tell me nothing I don't know. Just wish there was a way for folks to get educated and not stray from how they was raised and here the Lord been the comforter of your folk down...

ROSA: ...This doesn't mean you and me can't still be good, close friends.

VERA: ...through the generations and—and that alone gotta mean something—I may not be be so sophisticated in the eyes of the world, but that is a stone fact...

ROSA: Tell you what I'm...er...looking forward to—[*A beat.*] You and me being good buddies. Working together. Planning together. You and me settling Nana back here in her home, Mama. This whole thing bringing us together, Ma, me and you—

VERA: [*Indicating the Bible.*] Read it over once more, Ro— Sound it out like when you used to stand 'fore the Sunday School.

ROSA: I still see her on that stretcher...wheeled away—

VERA: Ro, now—Ro, nothing's gonna happen to your Nana. Now, you saw her, didn't you see her cleaned up, decent, safe and sound?

ROSA: Right, you right—hey and the fact of no broken bones— when the man said, "Just rest and she can come back home," ooh Momma! [*Referring to herself and clapping with relief.*] You talk about somebody wanting to sing and shout!

VERA: [*Smiling gratefully.*] On this very night at last—safe and sound at last, at last thank you Almighty God.

ROSA: [*Leaping up out of the bed exiting into the shadows as her voice trails off.*]...Now I have tomorrow's plan all worked out— [*She re-enters with her briefcase, and a phone directory.*]

VERA: [*Indicating the briefcase.*] Girl, that thing trails after you like afterbirth—and I wish you'd cut the cord!

ROSA: [*Smiling at* **VERA** *as she removes various pamphlets from her briefcase, showing them to* **VERA** *as she talks.*]...Had a brief talk with the hospital social worker—I dunno, where do they find these people? Couldn't answer half my questions to my satisfaction—so now after we check in on Nana in the morning— let's head out to Meridian County Social Welfare and get this homecare business straightened out...

VERA: [*She reads from Bible.*] "...Save me oh God for the waters are come in unto my soul..."

ROSA: [*Rosa takes a hair brush from behind the bed and begins brushing* **VERA**'*s hair.*] Momma, we need a—a pact with this situation, me and you—see, Uncle Way—Oh, he's a very good son to Ma Rose, held her together in this town, thirty years, nobody's denying him his due—but still, it's not like the woman understanding that you bring to this as the one daughter present.

VERA: [**VERA** *nods vigorously.*] I hear you—

ROSA: Right. And I can help you. The point is to get Ma Rose back home—I'm not above scheming if we have to—anything to get her to realize and accept that she can't live here alone—

VERA [*Suddenly* **VERA** *grabs the brush in* **ROSA**'*s hand and holds it. It is full of strands of hair.*] Ro, it's coming out—out, Ro.

ROSA: [*Reassuring* **VERA** *gently.*] No. No. No.

VERA [*Suddenly seeing* **ROSA**'*s hand.*] Girl, lookit them long and pretty fingernails!! [*Her voice drifting off to sleep.*] Guess you go to saunas and stuff like that, huh? [*Pause.*] Girl, am I beat. [*Pause.*] I guess the small-town homeboys 'round here and down at the plant—that kinda man—don't hold much interest for you.

ROSA: Well, hey—You got something there—Now why don't I while I'm here, just go down there and hang out and see who's available and hand out my business cards and—[*She stops at* **VERA**'*s expression.*] Just kiddin'—ha—don't look at me like that—Come on. [*Pause.*] Nothing wrong with the men 'round here but when you advance in life you get expectations, Momma, that just comes with the territory...I'm working on it...working on it—I just broke up with a very nice man.

VERA: Then why "broke up with"?

ROSA: Why is it you never remarried?

VERA: Me?

ROSA: All that time? It would have nice to have had some "rusty-butt" gentlemen...

VERA: [*Smiling.*] Watch you mouth—

ROSA: ...to hold me on his lap—somebody to catch you snuggling up to—

VERA: Talk sense—had m' little girl to raise—no time to be selfish 'bout myself.

ROSA: I was no excuse for you to have to give up sex.

VERA: [*Astonished at* **ROSA.**]
Will you hush—what's got into you!

ROSA: Mother—speak to me like you and any one of your women friends do! If we're going to be real friends—look—you see me and you think, "Oh, there's my V.P. daughter, there's my Rosa."—Fine, wonderful—let me really tell you—[*A pause.*] "Success" don't just come up to ring your doorbell—know what I mean? Success doesn't just all a-sudden decide to pay you a courtesy call, y'know what I'm saying? And I'm on the front lines each and every day—Mommy, then that fright can come on me without warning—I start thinking I don't "deserve" this position and I can't hold it—but still I stand for my people, I s'tand for the family—everybody's got a stake in where I'm at—But still I'm thinking, "God, don't let them find me out..." It's a trip to keep down this—this fear that in spite of my credentials, I could be this impostor, this total failure, this "jive"...

VERA: You just keep them newspaper clippings coming on back home—and whatever notice you get—wherever you speak and things, or whatever—no matter how small—I wanna know—

ROSA: Wheeled away—[*She blinks and shakes her head as if trying to cast out an image.*] When you wanna get a headstart on out to the Social Welfare in the morning, Ma?

VERA: [*Indicating the Bible.*] Here's one I wanna hear you on— and call it out to the air—like when you lead the youth choir—

ROSA: Momma, whatever's in your head is not me—[*A beat.*] Momma—Momma—Momma you remember all that time it took Nana to help me get over being scared of the dark? Well, it never took. I travel with my night light at all times—[*Laughs.*] still scared I might wake up in the middle of the night to the total dark, Momma.

VERA: Nonsense, you doing just fine—just fine. Why, this what's meant to be, Rosa—we just going through the trial of being apart of the line of generations—what we seeing with Ma Rose is jnst the cycle of life and we gotta bear up—we—er.

ROSA: Ma, you're gripping my hand—you're hurting me, Mommma.

VERA: Oh, pardon me—pardon me—er—I—

ROSA: [*Moving to wipe* **VERA**'*s tears.*] Here, lemme—

VERA: Quit. I'm okay—I'm fine—I'm just cold—dum old drafty house—

ROSA: Now she is curled up in her bed up at Crestwood...now she's warm and she can sleep...

VERA: Yeah! Yeah! Tell me more...tell me more...You picture Ma Rose and tell me...you talk it so well...

ROSA: She's all curled up in the hospital bed...it's all warm...she's been given the right dose of her medicine...Here, get down in the covers good...She resting calmly and safely...[ROSA *bends down to try to kiss and hug* **VERA**.]

VERA: [**VERA** *moves her head away, uncomfortably.*] Now-now we don't hafta get all mushy and carried away, now...that's okay. [**ROSA** *stops still, a flash of rage across her face.*] [*Looking up at* **ROSA**.] What?

ROSA: [*Smiling falsely.*] Nothing.

VERA: Keep talking...talk to me...talk to me...

ROSA: Uh-Hum...she's sleeping peaceful...nurses come in and check on her and make sure she's safe...Tomorrow we'll get there...we'll bring her flowers, bring a present...tell her about coming home this weekend, she'll be so happy...

VERA: Keep talking...keep talking...keep talking...[*Lights slowly fade.*]

★

monologue from
WAKING WOMEN
by Cassandra Medley

[*A second woman enters the stage and climbs onto the closed porch. She is* **ROSALIE**, *thin with a nervous, tremorous quality, a woman in her late 50's.* **ROSALIE** *is dressed in a crisp summer dress of the kind to indicate that "proper manners" is very important to her. She has a sorrowful expression on her face as she addresses the unseen woman before her. Throughout the monologue she speaks to the audience as if speaking directly to her close friend and confident,* **LUCILLE**.]

ROSALIE: Lucille now I hate to say this...but watch out if Olie-

Mae Johnson calls herself coming to view your husband. Let's hope she just stays at home, she's not that close to you is she? well I hate to say this but that woman just makes me so sick and discusted till I don't know what!

Girl, you ever heard Olie-Mae Johnson at a funeral? well be glad you ain't! She just gets to acting ole-timey and "colored"—ain't no other way to put it—she starts whooping and hollering and leaping and wailing and making a spectacle of herself at each and everybody's funeral—at folks funerals she don't *even* half way *know*—folks she done maybe spoke to once or twice in life, and don't know well enough to even tag a name to, let lone weep over! but yet and still when it gets to they funerals?! oh she gotta hog *all* the attention for herself!! I just hope she don't show up at your husband's cause she'll break down and carry on and moan and groan and collapse on the floor like she's part of your immediate family!! oooooh!! I get so *discusted* with that woman so till she makes it hard for me to recall I'm a Christian!! [*Pauses in thought.*]

Girl, I hope she don't show up on you....course now...ha...come to think of it....*may-be* if she *do* she might just surprise us and behave herself and conduct herself like she should—you 'member Sister Bodetta Price's funeral? [*Pauses.*] oh that was 'fore you joined our church. Well there was this Sister Price and she died and so okay, I call myself being neighborly and Christian and offering to pick up Olie-Mae at her house to drive her over to the funeral parlor to view the body.

Well I'm telling *you*!! I was so *discussed*!! here I drive up in front of Olie-Mae's place and I beep m'horn and she ain't even got out her own house good, fore here she come weeping and a-wailing something terrible!!! I say to myself, oh my goodness, *what* did I call myself doing offering to take this woman anywheres for??!! Oh you shoulda seen her—she couldn't even see her way to getting in my car, she was so broke up and grief-stricken!! she's so moaning and groaning and wailing! and I say to her I say, Olie-Mae *please*!! Will you *please* get a handle on yourself and stop acting like you been called to witness the Crucifixion!?

Oh she is carrying on something terrible, boo-hooing and ah blowing her nose and whatnot like she done lost blood kin and here she ain't even really *known* Bodetta Price. I'm telling you, I was so put out with that Olie-Mae Johnson, I didn't know what to do!

And I drive up to the funeral home and here I don't even get into the parking lot good, don't even get to even steer into the driveway—next thing I know Olie-Mae done flung open the door, flung herself out my car, and next thing I know, here Olie-Mae is flying through the doors of the funeral home, screaming and ah wailing and skreeching!! Here I ain't even got out of my car good and she's done gone shrieking through the reception room, gone screaming down one hallway and wailing up the other—turning this corner, tearing in through this room, flying down the aisle whooping and hollering, *flinging* herself onto the casket, wailing and wailing *then* she looks down and there's a bearded *white man* laying up inside there!!!

She looks up and there's this whole passel of white folks down on they knees, mouths hung open so wide they look like the wind's been knocked clean out of 'em they so shocked. Shocked at this wild and wet faced black woman who's come skreeching into they services, acting like ah reject from the insane asylum!!

Well sir, Olie-Mae was so embarrassed! So shamed fore the world, so pitiful! And I said to myself, well *good* for ya!!! you got that coming!!! that'll teach yah!! that'll learn you not to be putting on airs and exhibitions!! Thank you Jesus for shaming her low!!! good for her, that's justice!!! That'll keep her quiet!!

[*Fade Out.*]

★

scene from
THE WARNING—A THEME FOR LINDA
by Ron Milner

Ron Milner is currently living in Detroit, Michigan. Author of *What the Wine Sellers Buy*, Mr. Milner's other plays produced in New York include *Who's Got His Own*, presented at the American Place Theatre in 1966, and at the New Lafayette Theatre a year later. *The Warning—A Theme For Linda*, produced by Woodie King, Jr., at Tambellinis' Gate Theatre in Greenwich Village, was part of the *Black Quartet* which includes works by three other Black playwrights. *These Three* was produced at Concept East in Detroit, where Mr. Miller served as Artistic Director. Several of his short stories were included in anthologies such as *The Best Short Stories by Negro Writers* edited by Langston Hughes and *Black Short Stories* edited by Woodie King, Jr. His essays have appeared in *Black World*, *Negro Digest* and *Black Aesthetics*. He was a recipient of the National Endowment of the Arts Playwright's Grant in 1985. His most recent works were *Roads of the Mountain Top*, a theatrical portrait of Dr. Martin L. King, Jr., which was presented at the 1987 Dr. King National Holiday Celebration at the King Institute and *Checkmates* presented on Broadway in 1988/89 season.

SCENE: Dining room area. GRANDMOTHER sits at stage-right head of table; MAMA sits at rear-center seat to GRANDMOTHER's left, her bifocal glasses lying before her, pouring beer from Jumbo bottle into glass. GRANDMOTHER has arms folded atop table, watching her daughter with wry, derisive attitude. LINDA enters from archway, rear center, in green skirt, yellow overblouse, black high-heel shoes—fresh, healthy, lovely.

GRANDMOTHER: Well, well, all dressed up in high-heels, huh?

LINDA: [*Kissing her on forehead.*] Yep—Hey, Mama. [MAMA *gives slight nod, not looking.*] Give me a big juicy kiss. Uhh-'uh. [*Gives her one on cheek, hugging.*]

MAMA: [*Embarrassed.*] Girl!

GRANDMOTHER: [*Sarcastic.*] Watch out 'fore you make her spill somea' that mess. [**MAMA** *snorts and nods as though expecting this kind of comment.*]

LINDA: [*Going to stage-left head of table opposite* **GRAND-MOTHER**.] Just leave my mama alone. She can drink as much beer and get fat as she wants to.

MAMA: [*Looking straight ahead.*] I don't know what you mean, I ain't fat.

LINDA: [*Baby-talk.*] Aw, her ain't fat, Mama; her just a lil rolypoly, that's all, Mama. [*Playfully pinching her arm.*]

MAMA: [*Smiling in spite of self.*] Go on, Linda, girl: you crazy.

GRANDMOTHER: She mighty spry-hearted about somethin' or 'nother. You take your pill?

LINDA: [*Sighing.*] Yes, Grannie, I took my pill. [*Sipping.*] I don't know about them anti-hormone pills.

GRANDMOTHER: You should know about 'em. [**MAMA** *tries not to react.*]

LINDA: Grannie? Why you always try to talk so tough? You ain't nothin' but a big ol' wolf-hearted creme-puff. [**GRAND-MOTHER** snorts, looks away. As **MAMA** drinks beer.] Well, how was it out in those ol' rich Jew's house, Mama? How long did it take you to clean all those rooms with your slow, fat self? [**MAMA** *grunts, frowns.*]

GRANDMOTHER: She didn't do nothin' but iron a few pieces. An' took her all day to do that. I did all the real work—as usual.

MAMA: [*Looking, say, into glass.*] I don't like to iron nobody else's clothes.

GRANDMOTHER: Oh you don't, huh?

LINDA: Grannie, she didn't mean nothin', now.

GRANDMOTHER: I'm not talkin' to you, Miss Fast! You just shut up! You hear?! You been gettin' too lippy aroun' here lately. [LINDA *looks to* MAMA *who avoids all eyes.*] Just shut your mouth! I'm talkin' to your Mama! You jus' stay outta' it! [*To* MAMA]—So you don't like to iron nobody else's clothes, huh?

MAMA: Aw, Mama, now—

GRANDMOTHER: I guess you think I do like it, huh? Wash 'em and iron 'em, too! An' scrub somebody else's house, an' look after somebody else's kids! An' then have to come back here and look after yours! I guess you think I enjoy all that, huh?

LINDA: Grannie, please!

MAMA: [*Pouring more beer into not nearly empty glass.*] I just said I don't like to—

GRANDMOTHER: I heard what you said! An' I wish you'd said it 'fore you ask me for that beer.

LINDA: [*Trembling restrain't; tearful empathy.*] I don't see how you can talk to her like that, Grannie! Your own daughter! You know you can be awfully mean sometimes.

MAMA: Aw, Linda, don't play it no mind now. She don't—

GRANDMOTHER: Uh-huh, that's right; just don't pay me no mind. I ain't nobody aroun' here. But I'll tell you somethin', Miss Fast: I'll talk to her, you, and anybody else aroun' here! Any way I please! Just so long I'm tellin' the truth about 'em!—Now if that chokes you, get on up from the table! [*She and* LINDA *match glares;* LINDA: *breaks it off.*] You can't tell me what to do lil' ol' gal. Darn-tootin'. I'll talk about her. Don't like to do this. Can't do that! Everytime I get her job, or the people downtown get her a job—somebody get her one; cause she sure ain't gone get one for herself—what happens? Two three days—if that long—and she back in here on her behind waitin' for somebody to bring her a beer! [MAMA *calmly puts glasses on that too calmly sips beer.*]

LINDA: [*To feet.*] You know that even with her glasses she can't hardly see! She's always had trouble with her eyes! That's why she can't keep a job! And you know it too! You're just being mean! Pickin' at her!

MAMA: Linda jus' hush, now. Just leave it alone.

GRANDMOTHER: [*Guiltily backing off.*] Humph. Don't be rarin' up at me, lil' ol' gal.

LINDA: Well, just leave her alone! [*Slapping table as she sits back down.*]

MAMA: [*Calmly.*] Linda.

GRANDMOTHER: Humph. That's right: somebody better protect her. I'm gettin' too tired to do it, myself. Humph. But it ain't me you gotta' protect her from. Humph. Yes, I guess you got her trouble spotted all right. Never could see too clear. Always walkin' into what she shoulda steered clear of...Humph.

LINDA: What you tryin' to start now, Grannie, huh?

MAMA: [*Taking off glasses.*] Linda, don't you know that the more you talk the more she gone talk?

GRANDMOTHER: Naw, I don't feel like no whole lotta' talkin' I jus' wanna' know where's that no-good daddy of Paula's? When you gone put the people on his behind? [**LINDA** *sighs all eyes* **MAMA** *avoids all eyes.*] Causea' him layin' roun' here when he gets ready, that you can't get no mo' aid from the people. Yet, you can't never find him when it's time for him to do what he's supposed to. Where's he at, girl? When you gone get the people on him?

LINDA: [*Looking around as if for somewhere to spit.*] The people. The people!

MAMA: [*First real sign of harassment.*] Maybe he's workin' outta' town, on that man's truck. [**GRANDMOTHER** *snorts.*] I don't know! He usually brings it soon as he can! I don't want all that trouble.

GRANDMOTHER: What you think you got now?!—Bet he gets that other woman and her kids they money on time! Divorced! Of all the good Nigguhs in the world!

LINDA: [*In emotional knots.*] She's told you a hundred times she didn't know he'd been married! Didn't even know he had any kids until those—those people told her!

GRANDMOTHER: Didn't seem to make too much difference when they did.

MAMA: [*Matter of factly; sipping beer.*] Got to have somebody.

GRANDMOTHER: Yes! I guess you do! When you's as hot in the behind as everybody aroun' here is! [*Cutting glance at* **LINDA** *who looks away.*] An' you call that havin' somebody? Humph. Lord I gues that sure is your trouble all right. Turn you loose in the bank and insteada' the money you come out with the bags they keep it in! Lord, always been that way; ever since a kid. Always coming home with somethin' so beat-up and pitiful wouldn't nobody else even look at it.

MAMA: [*Rubbing eyes; sighing.*] Well, I guess that's the truth.

LINDA: Mama? You wanna' lay down for awhile?

GRANDMOTHER: I don't know what she got to be tired of: less it's them no-good Nigguhs.

LINDA: [*Standing.*] Come on, Mama. Why don't you?

MAMA: [*Straightening glasses.*] Naw, now, I don't wanna' lay down, now. I'm alright. Mama don't bother me.

GRANDMOTHER: Guess I don't; me and nothin' else.

★

scene from
THE WARNING—A THEME FOR LINDA
by Ron Milner

LINDA: [*After moment of returned glares.*] Well, Miss Thing? Miss Easy-Motion?

NORA: I better wait outside for Joan, 'fore you make me go in the kitchen and get me something an' there be blood all ova' these raggedy-ass flo's. [**LINDA** *snorts as* **NORA** *exits through archway.* **LINDA** *looks at mumbling, sleeping* **GRANDFATHER**, *puts bottle back on table; sits opposite him staring curiously for some moments.* **JOAN** *comes childishly steping back through room, casting baleful glare at* **LINDA** *before she goes out archway.*]

DONALD'S VOICE: Linda here? [**LINDA** *tenses; starts to brush at hair; stops impulse; stands watching entrance.*]

JOAN'S VOICE: Yeh, she's in there! [*For* **LINDA**'s *benefit.*] Wish you'd take her somewhere an' drown her! [**LINDA** *waits.* **DONALD** *comes in—wearing slacks, sport shirt, boot-shoes.*]

DONALD: [*Grinning, about to say something about* JOAN's *comment; but is taken aback by* **LINDA**'s *stoic expression.*] Hey—Uh—Somethin' wrong? [*Glances at* GRANDFATHER.]

LINDA: That's my Grandfather. He's—asleep. [*Shrugs.*] And drunk.

DONALD: Yeh, well: You drink enough an' you can make that. Look, some friends of mine are outside with a car. We're thinkin' about going out to Belle Isle; dig some trees and sky, you know. Nature awhile. Then there's a brother from the West Coast speaking over at the Black Arts hall tonight; with jazz and choppin' afterwards. We can have dinner in between.

LINDA: [*Stares impassively, for maybe four long beats. Important pause.*] I don't feel like going for a ride, or hearing any jazz.

DONALD: Naw? Well, what do you—I mean; why not?

LINDA: [*More long beats.*] I—I think I'm in love with you, Don. I've never felt like this about—about anyone before.

DONALD: [*Glancing at GRANDFATHER; smiling, shrugging; trying to joke over slight embarrassment.*] Oh, yeh? Well—Good. I mean you couldn't have picked a better cat. I mean, I really wouldn't have it any other way. You know? I mean—hell, I really don't know what to say, to that.

LINDA: [*Stares again; as his smile is replaced by curious stare.*] Don, can we go anywhere I want to? I mean, do you have any money? Will you take me anywhere I wanna' go?

DONALD: Uh—Yeh, Linda, baby. Where you wanna' go?

LINDA: [*Gives quick glance to GRANDFATHER, to archway.*] I wanna' go to a—a motel; [*Deep breath.*] or—or hotel; or whatever it is people go to—to make that happen. [*Deep breath.*] I wanna' get it over with. Get it started. Now. Tonight.

DONALD: [*Mouth hangs open; takes an involuntary half-step backwards; near whispers.*] Wha—? [*She look impassively.*]—you serious? [*She just looks, he glances at GRANDFATHER, at archway; goes to archway, look in hall. Comes back.*]—yeh, Yeh, lady. Yeh—Now! Damn. [*Sits down, looking at her.*] Yeh: you're serious. Yeh. Uh-huh. Well, okay. All right lady. Okay. Now you want me to—to leave now an'—an' come back later and—an' pick you up, right?

LINDA: [*Nodding, goes over to him; holding his face.*] I jus' want to ask you one thing, Don,

DONALD: What's that, lady?

LINDA: What are you going to be?

DONALD: Huh?—A writer. A damned good one, I hope.

LINDA: No, I don't mean that. I mean, are you going to be a man? A real man? A strong man? Because I'm going to be a real woman. And I can't be bothered with anything else.

DONALD: [*Looks a long moment; then stands, hands at her waist.*] Damn, baby—Yeh—You're straight-up and forever, ain't you! A tree! Damn. Yeh. [*Kisses her eyes.*] Yeh, I'll be here, around—around eight-thirty. [*Starts out, comes back; kisses her lips, looks, shakes head.*]

LINDA: Don?...[*He stops.*] You understand don't you? I don't mean just...in bed. Just that. Just there. I mean—be that, be there, everywhere. You understand?

DONALD: [*Pause.*] Yeh, Lady, I understand...Whatta' you think I am? [*Smiles, exits.*]

LINDA: [*Stares after him; then breathing deep, sits.*] Please, Don, please. Don't come unless you can give as much as I can. Please, Don, Please....

★

scene from
TELL PHARAOH
By Loften Mitchell

Narration was written by Gloria H. Anderson of the Compton, California school system.

CHARACTERS:
NARRATOR
MRS. BLACK, a middle aged woman
MISS BLACK, her Teen-age daughter
MR. BLACK, Sr., a middle aged man
MR. BLACK, Jr., his twenty year old son

NARRATOR: *Tell Pharaoh*, a concert drama, chronicles the history of the African American in New York City from the seventeenth century to the present. In 1626 when New York City was a Dutch outpost known as New Amsterdam, eleven African slaves were imported and housed on the fringe of what is now The Bowery. These eleven Africans built a wagon road to the upper part of the Settlement to a place called Haarlem, then spelled with two A's. Eighteen years later—with the support of rank and file White colonists, the Africans petitioned the Dutch for freedom, received it and settled in a swampland, which they built into a prosperous community. The community is today known as Greenwich Village....Mobsters crowded the streets, yelling Get Williams and Walker. These were the Black Broadway stars, Bert Williams and George Walker. Black comedian Ernest Hogan had to lock himself in a theatre overnight to escape a mob. This, then, frames the background for the scene you are about to witness. [*Now we see the front room of the* BLACK *apartment.* MISS BLACK *rushes in.*]

MISS BLACK: Mama! Mama!

MRS. BLACK: [*Rushes in.*] What is it, child? [*Then.*] Lord, my child been beat up again! Lemme look at you, girl.

MISS BLACK: Mama, I ain' hurt bad. Not as bad as one of them. I took off my shoe when them two White boys come up to me and said something nasty. And I parted one's hair with the heel of my shoe.

MRS. BLACK: [*Happily.*] You did??? [*Then.*] But, child, the Lord says you got to turn the other cheek.

MISS BLACK: I turned the other cheek, Mama—after I hit the other one with my fist and bloodied his nose.

MRS. BLACK: You did? That's good! [*Then.*] No! That's bad...Lord, I ain't never gonna get used to this North. I couldn't get used to down home, either. The Bible says you is supposed to love your neighbor, but They beat on us down there and up here they come in your house and beat on you. Lord, what we gonna do?

MISS BLACK: Mama, stop calling on The Lord 'cause He can get all confused if these White folks calling on Him to get rid of us while you calling on Him to help us!

MRS. BLACK: Girl, you shut your mouth! We already got White folks down on us, so don't go getting the Lord down on us, too!

MISS BLACK: I don't mind the Lord being down on us, 'cause He ain't beating on us like White folks is.

MRS. BLACK: He ain't gonna get a chance to beat on you 'cause if you keep on blaspheming His name, I'm gonna work on your backside 'fore He reaches you. I sure wish your Pa had a lived.

MISS BLACK: They'd a beat on him, too! How many nights did he come in here and kick over a chair or bang the wall? I used To lay in my bed and hear you all arguing about any little thing. One night I heard you tell him: "Go fight where you got mad"! And he told you: "If I did, you'd be a widow before you could bat an eye"! [*Then.*] Mama, I don't wanta stay here no more. I'm tired— tired of fighting to get in the front door, tired of walking the street and having men grab at me. This ain't what you and Papa walked all the way north for! If I don't do something about it, I ain't gonna be able to look you in the face or to even remember Papa for the man he really was!

MRS. BLACK: Yes, child! We going from here. A man come around the church the other day and he told us about apartments in Haarlem, renting to colored folks. Six room apartments for thirty-four dollars a month, with all modern conveniences except steam heat and bathrooms. Lots of colored folks talking about moving there. You think you'd like it.

MISS BLACK: Like it? Oh, Mama. please! Let's move. Move to where we can live like people and not be afraid. You can go out to your church groups and I won't have to meet you after, and maybe the boys can come around and see me one at a time and not have to tiring their friends to keep from getting jumped on on the way home. Mama let's move...[*They embrace. Then start out singing, "Getting Up Morning, Fare-thee-well, Fare-thee-well".*]

★

scene from
TELL PHARAOH
By Loften Mitchell

NARRATOR :And so the first Black families moved into Haarlem. To the land north of-110th Street came Southern Blacks escaping physical lynchings, West Indians escaping economic lynchings and Northern Blacks escaping lynchings in Lower Manhattan. They brought with them their religiosity, their folkways, mores and their dogged determination. During the 1920's there flowered in Harlem what came to be known as the Black Renaissance. The arts flourished. Whites journeyed to Harlem to visit night spots where jazz reigned supreme. The 1929 brought the Renaissance to an end. Unemployment was rampant and homeless, hungry people faced much of what we see today. But—the child of Harlem had the will to live, to survive, to make it. He knew his Black identity and in the 1930's he made up his own language which he threw into the faces of Whites, much as they resorted to Yiddish, Italian or Spanish...[*The scene is a Harlem street corner.* **MR. BLACK, SR.** *and* **MR. BLACK, JR.** *meet.*]

JUNIOR: Man. What you putting down?

SENIOR: I am putting down all skunks, punks and a *hard* hustle!

JUNIOR: Dad, I ain't dead and I am looking for some bread. I am like the bear. I ain't nowhere. I'm like the bear's brother, I ain't gonna get no further. In other words, I am like the Black night facing the White day. I am up tight and I don't want to stay that way!

SENIOR: You beating a dead horse to death 'cause I ain't no man of great wealth. If I'm lying, I'm flying. In fact, Jack if I'm lying, God's gone to Jackson, Mississippi and you know He wouldn't be hanging around in *that* place!

JUNIOR: You done come up crummy when I need you, Sonny. You have been a social hanger when I need a banger. You have low-rated me, ill-fated me, disgraced me and abraced me. I thought you was my main man and you have showed your can! You have been a drag and darn near a hag. You have brought me down, clown. You are supposed to be hip as a whip, but you are a crum, chum, and if I could afford a broom, I would sweep you off the scene, Gene!

SENIOR: You may be a poet and not know it. Go on, Gates, and solid swing, but I am forced to tell you just one thing: Your eyes may flash fire and you may spit, but none of my green bread you will git! [*They walk away from each other.*]

★

scene from
TELL PHARAOH
By Loften Mitchell

NARRATOR: From the depression came World War II,
then the cold War replaced the hot war.
And McCarthyism—It struck terror into the hearts and minds
of people everywhere. As bestiality displaced humanity,
And dissent was silenced—
A silence that made Korea a reality
That we buried yesterday, yet festers today
And becomes a running sore throughout our history!
America sought suburbia in the nineteen-fifties,
Leaving the cities for the impoverished and down trodden,
The displaced and the disadvantaged.
A new stereotype spread its wing and did to Harlem
What Black-faced comics had done to Black people long ago,
As though one had the plague!
But stubborn is the child of the African mother,
The most avid seeker of the American Dream,
Reaching, reaching
Believing always in tomorrow
And the Black Revolution thrust itself upon the scene,
A revolution as old as the nation.
In a small parish in Clarendon County, South Carolina
The Reverend J.A. DeLaine exhorted his followers:

SENIOR: Oh, the Voice of God has roared in my ears this terrible day, charging us with the duty of saving White children that they may grow up to be our brothers, of saving the lives of all those who have been taught hate instead of love. In the words of St. Paul: "When I was a child, I spake as a child, I thought as a child, I understood as a child, but when I became a man, I put away childish things. And now abideth Faith, Hope and Love, and the greatest of these is Love!"

MISS BLACK: Yes! Love!

SENIOR: Oh, yes! The Voice of God has roared in my ears, testing my faith—by letting them kill my beloved children—testing me as

Job was tested, as the Children of Israel were tested—as our people have been tested through nearly 300 years of slavery! Testing to see if God's work can be done on Earth as it is in heaven! And, oh, my friends, it will be done!

MISS BLACK: God's work will be done!

SENIOR: For even when the Law had been read and the signs that read 'This is for White' and 'This is for Black' have been burned, still shall there be lynch mobs, still there be deaths! There will be more testing, more suffering!

SENIOR: But, let not your heart be troubled, for the Seventh Seal shall be opened and they cannot hide!

MRS. BLACK: Ain't no hiding place down here!

SENIOR: And we cannot hide! We cannot hide by trying to kill the killers! For us to be worthy of our Great Duty us for us to teach them. Love on Earth—Soul! And how's that done?... Through Love! Yes, through Love! And where's that taught? In the home, in the Church, and in the Schools...And that's the real meaning there, for there's no such thing as being separate but equal. The only thing a man learns when he's separate is that he's not equal!...Oh, they've beat on us and called us ugly apes, and men in high places have tried to double-talk us and sell us down the river in the name of Expediency! But, this I know! No nation in history has truly lived when it has sold a person down the river! Kill any section of a people and you kill a nation!

MISS BLACK: Yes, Lord!

MRS. BLACK: Yes, indeedy!

JUNIOR: Preach on, Brother!

SENIOR: Old Pharaoh killed the Children of Israel and God sent Moses down to let His people go! Greece had its slaves and Greece fell!...A large percentage of pagan Rome was Jewish, but when the Church took over, the Jews were expelled—and Rome fell! Spain had its Inquisition and Spain fell! Czarist Russia had its pogroms and Russia fell! The English had their Irish, their Africans, their Asians and their islands of the sea—and England fell! America has had its Black people, its Latin people and its red people—and America has fallen! And the only way America can rise again is through you, my dark Brothers and Sisters! Will you give it a chance?

JUNIOR: Will it give me a chance?

SENIOR: It will have to because America likes to see others die, not Americans! And it's got to let us live for it to live! In my Father's house are many mansions. If it were not so, I would not have told you so...And that means there's Room for all—not up yonder in the sky, but here on Earth! For Black, yellow, brown, red, white or any other color. And I'm going to see to that! I'm going to see to that or go rotting in my grave!

THE GROUP: Yes, Lord!...Amen!...Amen! Amen!

ALL: [*Breaking into song.*] Keep your hand on the plow, hold on! Keep your hand on the plow, hold on! [*And they march off, singing, triumphantly.*]

★

scene from
TELL PHAROH
By Loften Mitchell

JUNIOR: [*In center stage.*] Somehow or other folks are just catching up to the fact that there was a Negro cowboy. If they'd bother to look they'd know that fifteen percent of America's cowboys were Black men. The baddest cowboy in the Old West was Black Sam. He was so bad that Webster had to look at him twice before he put the word 'bad' in the dictionary.

Well, this western town was quiet one Sunday morning. You could smell the coffee brewing and the bacon frying, and from every house you could hear the chatter of folks as they put on their Sunday-go-to-meeting clothes for church. Suddenly—on top of the hill outside town there rode up this big Black cowboy. He was riding a bear. He rode that bear right on into town and stirred up so much dust that the town got quiet, the coffee stopped brewing, the bacon stopped frying, and houses got quiet because everybody and his brother got out of that town. It was so deserted that tumbleweeds flew up and down that town's street, crying about being so lonely.

This Black cowboy rode that bear right up in front of the town saloon. He told the bear to Whoa! and he got off it, wrapped his big hands around the bear's neck, choked it, then flung it across the street. Then he started into the saloon. He was so big he couldn't get into the door. He was seven feet tall and he weighed 475 pounds. He walked right on through the door, pulling off half the wall and half the ceiling. He brushed the dust from his shirt and walked up to the people who hadn't run out of town. Both stood, trembling, 'cause they knew this was Black Sam, the baddest cowboy in the Old West. The Black cowboy ordered a bottle of red-eye and he broke the top of the bottle and poured down the liquor down again. He wiped his mouth and the sheriff trembled and decided he'd better get on the good side of Black Sam. He looked up at the Black cowboy and said: "What about another bottle of red-eye on me?"

The Black cowboy shook his head and wiped some more liquor from his mouth and said: "No, thanks. I got to get out of town before Black Sam gets here!"

MRS. BLACK [*As Junior returns to lectern.*] All of this Pharaoh has denied us, and we search for it and our identity while he seeks untold wealth in undreamed of forms, While we seek yet the story of Long Island, Brooklyn, the Bronx, Westchester, Soul City, and the heroic souls who built these communities. We seek yet to plant our feet on this earth, to discover it, when this earth no longer has a meaning For Pharaoh is reaching for the stars!

MISS BLACK: [*Crying out.*] Pharaoh! Who is he? [*Scene.*]

★

scene from
TATUM FAMILY BLUES
by Charles Michael Moore

Mr. Moore is based in Chicago and is a visiting artist for Urban Gateways. He has served on the Chicago Council on Fine Arts, Pegasus Players for the Young Playwrights Festival and Piney Woods School in Mississippi.

Other plays which have been produced include *Roommates*, by Four Star Theatre in L.A., *Love's Light In Flight* at ETA Theatre. That play was selected as "Pick of the Decade."

Love's Light was also produced at the Madame Walker Theatre in Indianapolis. *The Hooch* was produced at the New Federal Theatre in New York as well as ETA Theatre. His *One Nickle on This Wine* has been published by the Illinois State Press and his production *Say-Rah* was nominated Best New Work and Choreography. It also won a Jefferson Wing Citation.

The American College Festival gave Moore a Library Award for *And That's The Way It Was, Walte*.

TONY: [*He is in the middle of a story that has* **MELODY** *rolling in laughter.*] I'm not lying, Melody, one gym shoe. And his other foot was bare. Wardlow didn't even have time to put a sock on his foot. And Florence was running behind him, beating him with a wooden spoon in one hand, and swinging a butcher knife at him with the other one. I'll kill you. I'll stab you with this old rusty butcher knife...

MELODY: Tony quit...

TONY: I swear to Seventh Heaven. Me and Mama was coming up the road when we saw it happen. Florene didn't have on nothing but that old raggedy faded blue house coat of hers that wasn't even buttoned up right. Half her hair was in rollers and the other half was sticking straight up in the air. She looked like, "who shot John in the pantry." Mama was so embarrassed...

MELODY: What? That sister of ours was a trip.

TONY: Was a trip?

MELODY: Now, now, be nice.

TONY: Tell Florene to be nice. She was crazy then and even more crazy now. Dad says she watches too much television and ends up trying to act like the people on it.

MELODY: Dad still doesn't watch television?

TONY: Sports. He even got cable TV so he can see the Chicago Cubs play...Melody, is this true? Florene said that you used to think I was your baby when I was born.

MELODY: Uh, she did, huh?

TONY: Yeah, and how you and Mama used to fight over me.

MELODY: Well, Tony we're talking about some strange times back then.

TONY: But how could I be your son?

MELODY: Her, that was the question that bugged the hell out of Mama, too. Well, I may as well bring it all out since that's what I'm here, for. What do you know about the vision?

TONY: You mean like two take away one?

MELODY: No, not division. I mean *The* Vision. Dad's vision.

TONY: Uh, you mean Dad's Vision. Man, I haven't heard anybody talk about that for a long time.

MELODY: You haven't?

TONY: Naw, not since they had that fight.

MELODY: Since who had what fight?

TONY: Uh, you don't know about that either, do you? I had to pull them off of each other, me and Florene. Melody they all day long. Throwing pots and pans and plates...I got hit in the head with a cookie sheet...

MELODY: Daddy and Mama?!

TONY: But the knot on my head wasn't as big as the one on Dad's head! You could see his knot from the other side of the room. Ma had a bruise on her arm. They was serious.

MELODY: Tony, wait a minute. Mom and Dad? What were they fighting about?

TONY: Dad's Vision. And Mama's Church. I had to fix my own dinner. And I wasn't but ten. Florene wouldn't even fix me nothing.

MELODY: So, what happened?

TONY: I almost burned the skillet up trying to fix me a pork chop sandwich.

MELODY: No...

TONY: Oh, uh, Dad messed around and hit Mama too hard, I think he slapped her, and she called the Sheriff.

MELODY: Oh no, Tony...

TONY: It was a mess. You missed a good one. But I'll tell you one thing, we never heard about that vision, anymore. Dad just goes fishing, and Mama just goes to church. I have to keep them both company.

MELODY: They don't do anything together?

TONY: They both complain about Florene's kids. So, what about it? What's Dad's Vision got to do with me being your baby?

MELODY: I was obsessed by it. Guess I still am. Anyway what you've talking about is back when I was 15. I thought I was pregnant, and nobody could tell me anything different.

TONY: Pregnant with me?

MELODY: No, not you. It's just that all of a sudden I became pregnant. Never had been with a man, or anything like that, but I was pregnant.

TONY: Man, I bet Mama really tripped out.

MELODY: She took me to Reverend Curry to have me exorcised.

TONY: Reverend Curry? [*He chuckles.*] You know he's dead, now. Dad said he ate himself to death...

MELODY: He was fat then, too. And so, Mama told Reverend Curry that he needed to work with me because I was thinking evil thoughts—I needed to be prayed for. He told her, he said, "Uh, Sister Tatum, it is my sincere belief..."

TONY: That sounds just like him, too.

MELODY: "...I truly believe you need to take this child to the colored fambly doctor over up at the County Seat. Because it is my *august* opinion, that it's more than evil thoughts what got her belly swelled up like it is..."

TONY: Then you really was pregnant...

MELODY: Tony, seriously, my mind had convinced my body, I had convinced myself, that I was pregnant. And I took on all the symptoms of pregnancy. [*Almost whispers.*] Including my cycle. I didn't have a period for three months...

TONY: Ooooh. How did you do that? What did the Doctor say?

MELODY: Oh, he thought I was crazy. "Young lady, you say you never had sex, you've never been touched by a boy, or a man, and yet you're going to claim you're preanant. I think you ought to cut the foolishness. You are no more pregnant than I am."

TONY: So, why did you think you was pregnant?

MELODY: Because of Dad's vision. Tony, inside of me was another Immaculate Conception.

TONY: A what?

MELODY: Immaculate Conception. Remember Sunday School? Virgin, having a baby...?

TONY: Oh, yeah...

MELODY: ...I believed that God had touched me inside, and started growin right there...I'm serious. I could feel, you could even see the baby kicking. Ask Mama. She got scared to be around me. Went to a lot more prayer meetings, and love feasts just to get away. And Daddy, he didn't know what to do. See, he knew the power of what was happening. His vision called for this but at the same time, see he still loved Mama. Even though they were arguing all the time, they still loved each other. She got pregnant. You came along.

TONY: Yeah, Tony T. to the rescue...

MELODY: Rescue my foot. Mama went off when she got pregnant. Talking about violent, you think Florene acted up with Wardlow, you shoul have seen Varianne Josephine Tatum in action. Came in one night when I was asleep in the bed, had one of them doubled leather razor straps, and made up her mind she was going to beat that devil out of me. Tony...I think I still walk with a limp from that. Dad almost couldn't get her off of me.

TONY: It was rough, huh sis?

MELODY: Rough?! Shoot...I never felt so alone in my life. My baby felt it, too. I could hear him crying inside me. I felt it when he turned around and left me...

TONY: Turned around and left you? What do you mean, left you?

MELODY: Wherever he came from, he went back.

TONY: What?

MELODY: Daddy can explain it better than me. But, see Tony, that's not really the point. The point is, what happened was, as soon as my baby was completely gone, you, in Mama's stomach, kicked her for the very first time. You had never moved before that moment. Ask her. Ask Mama. Never moved before that moment. Ask her. Ask Mama.

TONY: Then you know what? That means...Mama! [*He broadly hugs her as they laugh.*]

MELODY: Get off me, you big head...

TONY: Don't cha love me, Mommy...?

MELODY: Quit, Tony...[*We hear* MRS. TATUM's *voice off stage in the front room.*]

★

scene from
THE HOOCH
by Charles Michael Moore

SCENE: Viet Nam, during the war, in a US Army barracks. There
has been an incident in which one of the soldiers has been killed.
Later that afternoon.

[**BROWN** and **HOLLOWAY** *enter with heads hung low.*
HOLLOWAY *sits down at his rack, offers* **BROWN** *a cigarette,*
and lights one up himself. **BROWN** *proceeds to the doorway near*
PRIDE'*s rack and smokes his cigarette.*]

HOLLOWAY: You know whose fault it is, don't you?

BROWN: [*Only half hearing him.*] What?

HOLLOWAY: It's that new guy's fault. If anybody is to blame
for what happened to Pride...

BROWN: How you sure?

HOLLOWAY: None of this would of happened, if Promus had a
been where he was s'posed to be.

BROWN: I'm the one who told Willie to go up on the hill. He
was following my orders.

HOLLOWAY: Brown, what is wrong with you? Ever since that
dude's been here, you been making excuses for him. Hell, just
because he's Black don't make him one of us.

BROWN: Us, what?

HOLLOWAY: Grunt, infantry, the real deal...

BROWN: Holloway, you took the test to change your M.O.S. and
join up with the Air Wing!

HOLLOWAY: Aw, you remember how that went down...

BROWN: And you flunked the test all three times that you took it.

HOLLOWAY: They didn't want me in there cause they know I ain't no tom.

BROWN: So, now Promus is a tom, huh? Hollowhead, don't say nothing to me because you're just jealous of the dude.

HOLLOWAY: Well, I'll just be damned. I ain't said nothin' about...

BROWN: You ain't got to say nothing when you show it as much as you do. You even show it around them...Now, I think Promus is sincere, I think he's dedicated, and I think there's something special about him. Now, Willie Pride, I love, loved Willie Pride, but I knew all the time that if you fucked up as much as he did, it's bound to come back at you. I know there's reason why Pride ain't here, now.

HOLLOWAY: Yeah, Earnest Promus. Brown, you're wrong, man. I ain't jealous of that dude. I just don't trust him.

BROWN: Why? Cause he's radar? Cause he's up on that hill? Let me tell you something, Holloway, Position is the key. We need somebody up on that hill. We need somebody who knows what they're looking at up on that hill. Do you?

HOLLOWAY: I almost passed that last test...

BROWN: Holloway, you ain't thinking straight. All you're thinking about is you. Same way you be acting about them sisters back home, You're jealous of them, scared of them, and insecure in dealing with them. It's I, I, instead of we.

HOLLOWAY: Hey Brown—climb off of me!

BROWN: Naw, you done made me mad! You been over here in this war almost a year and ain't learned nothing yet. I'm beginning to wonder why I let you in on my operation in the first place.

HOLLOWAY: Operation? What's this got to do with the operation? We're sending a bunch of damned marijuana seeds back to the states. What's that got to do with Promus?

BROWN: We are sitting on top of a gold mine, Hollowhead. All that land my Granddaddy got down south is just waiting to go to work.

HOLLOWAY: Brown, Brown, growing reefer in the states is against the law, remember?

BROWN: It is now, yeah. But, they got to make it legal, I heard they already been making plans.

HOLLOWAY: Says who?

BROWN: Ask Blankenship. Hell, the point is, what I'm trying to say is, self control, John Holloway, that's what I'm talking about, self control. We can't get it fighting amongst ourselves. We gotta unite to fight with all our might, brother. Twenty four hours a day. Can you dig where I'm coming from?

HOLLOWAY: Yeah, yeah, okay! [*They settle down.*] I, uh, found a joint in my flack jacket. Wanna fire it up?

BROWN: [*He takes it, lights it, and walks to the door looking out.*] 'Bout damn time...

HOLLOWAY: What? [*He joins him.*]

BROWN: Sun's going down Wow, look at that sky. All them colors coming together. This is my favorite time of the day over here. Can't stand all that sunlight. Got used to the heat. But the light? Too powerful. Light on top of light...

HOLLOWAY: Enough to drive you mad.

BROWN: Yep. If you let it. What can a mad man do, though? Got to learn how to deal with the light.

HOLLOWAY: Just gotta use more than your eyes to see it with.

BROWN: Yep...You know what, Holloway? You ain't as dumb as you look, sometimes...Aw, hell...

HOLLOWAY: Somebody coming?

BROWN: Yeah, old Blank and shit.

HOLLOWAY: He's cool.

BROWN: Naw, the fool's been drinking. [**BEE** *can be heard singing, "The Green, Green Grass Of Home," by Tom Jones.*]

BEE: [*Not noticing the men as he enters,* **BEE** *continues to sing as he goes to his rack and sits. He finishes the song, sees the men, and speaks.*] Yep, we lost a good one there, didn't we?

HOLLOWAY: Pride?

BEE: A great guy. Willie Pride was truly a great guy. Could chug-a-lug a pitcher of beer in one swallow...great guy...

HOLLOWAY: [*Nonchalant.*] He was alright...

BEE: Oh, I know what you guys are doing. You're trying to be cool about it, right? Right, Brown?

BROWN: That's the hazards of war. Ain't nothing guaranteed.

BEE: Nothing guaranteed. You know I really admire you guys to do that. No, I'm serious, now. I really, really do. It takes a lot of balls to go out there fighting for your life everyday...

BROWN: It's called survival.

BEE: And then you can sit around and shoot the shit like nothing has happened. I wish I was one of you...

HOLLOWAY: A brother?

BEE: No, a grunt...Lot of balls...[*Notices his.*] Hey John, I need to take a little run to the village. How about you?

HOLLOWAY: Mess with them women? I ain't got no cash?

BEE: [*Pulls out a wad of "funny money."*] No sweat, G.I.

HOLLOWAY: Why not? [*They prepare to leave.*]

BROWN: Where the hell you going?

HOLLOWAY: Take a walk. I'll be back.

BROWN: Aw, fool, risking your ass again for some leg.

HOLLOWAY: Yellow fever, blood. Go 'head and finish this. [*Hands him the joint.*]

BROWN: Holloway...

HOLLOWAY: Got to do something, Brown. You know that. [*He and* BEE *exit.*]

BROWN: You about the dumbest...[*Heading to his rack.*] "Two weeks to fight, yeah..." [*At Willie's rack.*] Willie Pride, I'm sorry brother, but I gotta get you off my mind...[*He goes to his rack. From inside the hooch, inside* BROWN'S *mind,* VOICES *are heard. They almost sound like children.*]

VOICES: Trick or treat.

BROWN: [*He looks around the room, then at the joint.*] Um, um, um...

VOICES: Trick or treat. [BROWN *gets serious.*] Trick or treat.

BROWN: [*Picks up his rifle.*] You can play your games if you want to, but I ain't got time for them [*The right door flies open. Brown jumps up on his rack preparing to do battle. The two* **SERVANTS** *of* **HEE** *enter the room. They bear on a stretcher a human body covered with a sheet. They are the* **VOICES**.]

VOICES: Trick or treat, trick or treat, trick or treat...[*They place the stretcher on* **SEEBOLD'***s rack.* **HEE** *enters.* **HEE** *wears a Black beret, and a Black glove on his right hand.* **HEE** *is the distortion of a Black Militant.*]

HEE: What's happening, Brother Brown?

BROWN: Old man.

HEE: I have something for you.

BROWN: [*Holds up rifle.*] I got something for you, too.

HEE: Brother Brown, put that thing away. It is totally useless against me, and you know it.

BROWN: Yeah, I guess it is. Got my wars mixed up. What you want?

HEE: I want to be your friend. I brought you a present.

BROWN: I don't want anything from you. Ain't you got that straight yet, old man? I don't want to be your friend, okay? [*The* **SERVANTS** *step in.*] And keep your monkeys off of me...

HEE: Let him be. We have come in peace. Relax yourself, Brother Brown.

BROWN: I ain't got time to. What do you want?

HEE: Trick or treat. [**HEE** *gestures to the body and it sits up. The sheet falls from it's face to reveal* **PRIDE**. *He calls out in pain.*]

PRIDE: Brown, help me Brown...

BROWN: Willie! Oh man...

HEE: Look at him. This is your friend. I brought your buddy to you.

BROWN: Get him out of here.

HEE: What's the matter? Can't you look at him? I thought it would please you to have one last look. Go ahead, talk to him...[HEE *allows* PRIDE *to speak.*]

PRIDE: It hurts, Brown. It hurts so bad. Please, help me...

BROWN: Get him out of here!

PRIDE: Brown, please. Please listen to me.

BROWN: I can't. I can't help you, Willie.

PRIDE: Talk to me, Brown. When you talk to me, the pain don't hurt so bad.

BROWN: I don't know what to say, Willie. I can't help you...! [HEE *makes* PRIDE *yell out in pain.* BROWN *rushes to him.*] Where does it hurt, buddy? Where is the pain.

PRIDE: My back. My back hurts so bad. It hurts all the way through, Brown.

BROWN: [*To* HEE.] Why are you doing this to him? He's already dead. Why don't you let him rest?

PRIDE: Listen to me, Brown. I asked Hee to bring me back here. I knew it would hurt, hurt both of us, but I had to talk to you again. I want you to help me.

BROWN: How Willie? What can I do?

PRIDE: LISTEN! I saw that radar set. Seebold let me see it. He showed me everything up on that hill, like it was important that he show me. I couldn't figure out why. He didn't really want to show me, but he did. I told him I didn't understand, but...then we started down the hill. Had forgot all about looking for Promus. We started down the hill, and I heard Seebold laughing. I looked around to see what was so funny, and there was that rifle staring me dead in my face. He was crazy Brown, like a mad man. Told me to get off his mountain, I didn't belong there. I said, "Man, what is wrong with you?" But it was too late. I knew I'd better run, and that's what I tried to do. I ran as fast and as hard as I could until that pain came in my back. It hurt me so bad that it knocked me down. I called for you Brown. I knew you would help, but you weren't around. Then, the sun went down, the pain went away, and I went to sleep...

BROWN: Seebold shot you?

PRIDE: I knew I should of stayed back there and fought him like you would have, but, I was scared, Brown. I was scared. I thought he was on my side. I thought...

BROWN: Why that dirty Mother...yeah, okay, I'll get him for you buddy. Don't worry, I'll get that motherfucker...

PRIDE: No, Brown. Don't do that. That's not what you do...

BROWN: Say what? [**HEE** *snaps to attention.*]

PRIDE: That's what HEE wants you to do. Don't...[**HEE** *silences* **PRIDE** *and makes him groan in pain.* **PRIDE** *fights to talk, but can't.*]

BROWN: Willie, what did you say? Speak to me, Willie...

HEE: He has nothing more to say.

BROWN: Let him talk! Or are you scared of what he might say? It's not Willie that wants me to kill Seebold. It's you. [**HEE**

gestures and **PRIDE** *yells out.*]

HEE: Listen to that, brother Brown. That is what you need to hear...Listen to your friend, as he dies...I know you, Brown, I know that you must destroy this Seebold. You cannot let him get away with this.

PRIDE: [*To the surprise of* **HEE** *and his* **SERVANTS, PRIDE** *speaks.*] Fight him, Brown, fight him...

HEE: [**HEE** *turns the situation around.*] Yes, Brown, fight him, kill him, destroy this Seebold...

BROWN: Why should I listen to you?

HEE: Listen to me? It is not I that wants to kill Seebold, it is you. I brought you your buddy. I am your BROTHER!

BROWN: You are not my brother.

HEE: Think about what has happened. Pride is dead, Seebold killed him. That White guy, that honky, killed our brother. We aren't Tom-ing out, are we...? What are you going to do about it?

BROWN: I have no choice, do I?

HEE: The decision is yours.

BROWN: Yeah, yeah it is.

HEE: Sleep...[**HEE** *gestures and* **BROWN** *crumbles to the floor, asleep.* **HEE** *Gestures to the* **SERVANTS** *and they cart* **PRIDE** *away who fell asleep the moment* **BROWN** *did...To* **BROWN.**] You fool. [**HEE** *laughs as he exits* .]

★

monologue from
FOREVER MY DARLIN'—A Play With Music
Daniel Walter Owens

Playwright Dan Owens was born, raised and educated in Malden, Massachusetts. While residing in Roxbury, Massachusetts, Mr. Owens had his plays produced and performed by the New African Company, the People's Theater of Cambridge and the Elma Lewis School. Mr. Owens also wrote shows which were produced for local television in Boston by Ms. Alice Myatt (*Mizizi Roots*) and Mr. Steve Hussein (*Brotherlove*).

While living in New York City, Mr. Owens has had his works produced by The New Federal Theater, The Frederick Douglass Creative Arts Center, The Negro Ensemble, The Afro-American Studio Theater, The Theater of Universal Images (Newark, New Jersey), The Richard Allen Center for Culture and the Arts (RACCA), The George Street Playhouse (New Brunswick, New Jersey) and the Westport Summer Playhouse (Westport, Connecticut).

The produced plays of Mr. Owens include: *Emily T, Sandra Lane, Not, The Michigan, Lagrima del Diablo, The More You Get—The More You Want (a musical), Del, Bargainin' Thing, Les Noirhommes, The Box, Little Ham (a musical) and Forever My Darlin'* (a play with music).

Mr. Owens was twice a participant in the Eugene O'Neill National Playwrights Conference (Waterford, Connecticut), the recipient of a Rockefeller Grant for Playwriting and a recipient of a grant from the fund for New American Playwrights—the Kennedy Center for the Performing Arts.

Mr. Owens currently lives in Seattle, Washington with his wife and daughter.

TAMMY: Thanks for takin' me home last night, Francine....But you should have let me kick that heifer's behind. Let 'em call the police! Sonny showin' up at Bootsie's party like that with her Him makin' me feel like...like [*Beat.*] We was goin' to get married, Smooch, I mean Francine. Well, Sonny, didn't exactly ask me 'n' all. Not like Nelson asked you. But we talked about it. Marry. Have kids. He was goin' to be mine forever. "Forever Darlin'." That's what he used to say. "It's always goin' to be me and you baby.Always and forever." He'd say that to me every time we...we...People think I'm fast, Francine. Even you think I'm fast. [*Bitter laugh.*] "Ole Fast Tammy Browne!" And your sister JoAnne just *knows* I'm fast. Hell, Tookie faster than me! [*Laughs.*] Tookie, faster than everybody! [*Beat.*] I'm not fast, Francine. I'm not. More mouth than anything else. Only been with one other boy 'sides Sonny. Only one!! [*Beat.*] Sonny didn't have to show up at that party with her. He knew I was goin' to be there. He didn't have to do it! Don't you hear what I'm sayn' to you? Sonny's left me!

★

scene from
FOREVER MY DARLIN'—A Play With Music
by Daniel Walter Owens
_____

CHARACTERS:
    FRANCINE LINCOLN
    AUNT DORIS
    TAMMY BROWNE
    JOANNE LINCOLN
    NELSON DANDRIDGE
    TOOKIE [The same actress who plays JOANNE can also
        play TOOKIE.]
_____

[JOANNE *is unpacking from a suitcase on her bed, she is putting clothes in the closet and in a drawer open in the dresser...* FRANCINE *is putting the records in boxes...*]

JOANNE: [*Derisive laugh.*] You don't know who Thurgood Marshall is?

FRANCINE: Thurgood who?

JOANNE: Thurgood Marshall!

FRANCINE: Never heard of him.

JOANNE: Never heard of the United States Supreme Court either, I bet.

FRANCINE: Do they sing the "blues?"

JOANNE: Funny...The girl thinks she has a sense of humor

FRANCINE: Bet you don't know what is happening in Houston, Texas tonight?

JOANNE: Thurgood Marshall won a case for us. Well not just for us but for—

FRANCINE: Johnny Ace is singing in Houston, Texas tonight.

JOANNE: Thurgood Marshall argued a case before the United States Supreme Court, and he won! We won!

FRANCINE: Wish I was going to be in Houston tonight...

JOANNE: Here I am trying to educate you...trying to tell you something important, and you are talking about some rusty ole conk headed darkie of a rhythm 'n' blues singer.

FRANCINE: Johnny Ace is not rusty and he is not a darkie and I bet more people heard of him than your Thurgood Marshall. Does he sing?

JOANNE: You're hopeless. She is hopeless.

FRANCINE: Don't forget to call your Aunt.

JOANNE: I don't feel like calling anyone, I don't feel like speaking to anyone. Spending half my life on that train.

FRANCINE: JoAnne...

JOANNE: It left Union Station on time. Sat outside Providence for three hours because some fool decides to end it all the day before Christmas. People better stop dying and having emergencies around holidays, that's all I know.

FRANCINE: Girl, you—

JOANNE: Uncle Willis dying Thanksgiving Day. Dropping dead right at the table before Daddy even cut the turkey. Then Mama's Daddy having a heart attack just three days before Christmas. Folks should be more considerate!

FRANCINE: I'm sure they are choosin' when to die.

JOANNE: I have to change my plans at the last minute and take the train home the day before Christmas. I could have been home. Daddy and Mama were supposed to pick me up on their way back from North Carolina.

FRANCINE: Tell me something I don't already know.

JOANNE: Grandpa having that heart attack.

FRANCINE: Poor JoAnne.

JOANNE: I had to carry all my gifts and my laundry.

FRANCINE: You forget how to use a washing machine?

JOANNE: And here we are left with Daddy's crazy sister to take care of us.

FRANCINE: Mama and Daddy will be back tomorrow night.

JOANNE: Christmas will be over. See you got Uncle Willis' band outfit hanging up in our closet.

FRANCINE: Yeah...

JOANNE: His pork pie hat hanging over your headboard.

FRANCINE: That was there before you left for school, JoAnne.

JOANNE: Still have that photo of you, me, and him taken at the beach.

FRANCINE: 'Course I do, You have one too.

JOANNE: Girl, what are we going to do about this room?

FRANCINE: This room?

JOANNE: It needs a change.

FRANCINE: JoAnne, you been talkin' to Aunt Doris?

JOANNE: It's been looking this way for—

FRANCINE: And it will continue to look this way.

JOANNE: It needs to be painted. All this junk needs to be thrown out. It needs a different feel...a different look. It needs—

FRANCINE: It needs you to leave it the hell alone!

JOANNE: It's a kid's room.

FRANCINE: And we are "miss grown?" JoAnne, this room is us. It is you and me.

JOANNE: It may be you but it damn sure isn't me.

FRANCINE: This is your bed. You are unpacking and putting your clothes in the drawers in that dresser. You are hanging clothes in that closet. Your side of it.

JOANNE: The room needs to be stripped. It needs—

FRANCINE: Don't you have a dorm room down at Howard?

JOANNE: I will be coming home...sometimes. I will have to sleep in this room. [*She sniffs the air.*] It even has an old smell.

FRANCINE: That old smell is your upper lip

JOANNE: Get rid of all this. Those photos of Johnny Ace. That hat. That saxophone.

FRANCINE: You can do what you want with your side but my side stays the same.

JOANNE: [*At the dresser she opens another drawer and is about to put in something when she suddenly yells out.*] Francine!

FRANCINE: What!?! [*Startled.*]

JOANNE: My sweater! [*She lifts a sweater from the drawer.*]

FRANCINE: Sweater!?!

JOANNE: Yes sweater.

FRANCINE: So...

JOANNE: This big red spot.

FRANCINE: Barbecue sauce. It'll wash out.

JOANNE: Not before tonight's Christmas party.

FRANCINE: JoAnne, you have other sweaters.

JOANNE: All the sweaters I have don't go with my plaid pleated skirt.

FRANCINE: Then wear another skirt.

JOANNE: And look! It's all stretched out off shape by those watermeons you call—

FRANCINE: Why, JoAnne!

JOANNE: Bobby is going to be at that party tonight.

FRANCINE: Good for him.

JOANNE: He gave me this sweater last Christmas

FRANCINE: So.

JOANNE: It was going to be special and all, me wearing the sweater.

FRANCINE: Wear another sweater JoAnne.

JOANNE: You are a pain in the behind.

FRANCINE: Bet that isn't what ole Bobby says to you. What did you gave him last Christmas? What are you going to give him this Christmas?

JOANNE: None of your damn business.

FRANCINE: [*Mocking tone.*] "Come on, JoAnne. Just a little."

FRANCINE: [*She switches voices.*] No, Bobby. No...I can't. I'm saving myself for my husband. [*She switches volces again.*] Aww JoAnne. Please. Please. Pretty please. [*She laughs.*]

JOANNE: [*She balls the sweater up and throws it at* **FRANCINE**] Simple, Simple. You a simple ass!

FRANCINE: Why, JoAnna!

JOANNE: [*This builds in emotion.*] You had no right wearing my sweater!

FRANCINE: Then you should have taken it down to Ole Howard U.

JOANNE: It was a gift to me, it was my present. You had no right going in my things. It's mine. Mine! [*She starts to cry.*]

FRANCINE: [*Taken aback by* **JOANNE'S** *outburst.*] Dog, JoAnne...It's only a sweater, Almost out of style at that. I'll buy you another sweater.

JOANNE: [*Sobbing.*] With what?

FRANCINE: Well, when I—

JOANNE: [*Sobbing-laughing.*] When you make it big? When you and your group sing at the Apollo?

FRANCINE: We will. We have chance now to...

JOANNE: And look at this room. Where Johnny Ace leaves off Uncle Willis takes up.

FRANCINE: [*Conciliatory.*] There's plenty of room for you to put up photos and—

JOANNE: Uncle Willis. Johnny Ace. Uncle Willis. "Your" Uncle Willis. Anyone think that you were the only family member at the funeral. You were the only one who hurt. You were the only one mourning. The rest of us were so worried about you when did we get time to mourn...when did we get time to deal with our hurt? Hell, I had to be alone in my dorm room at school. I had no one there for me. No one to hold me. I was alone Francine. Alone. [*She takes up the framed photo of her,* **FRANCINE**, *and* **WILLIS**.] I had a photo like this. Me, you, and Uncle Willis. I had one until I ripped it up.

FRANCINE: JoAnne why would you—

JOANNE: You mourn one way. I mourn another. [*Pause.*] I am home, Francine. It is Christmas and I am home. And I am not here to mourn or be reminded of mourning since I couldn't before. So this room has to change. And it will. Before I go back to Howard. Before the New Year comes. This room will change.

★

monologue
GOOD BLACK
by Rob Penny

Rob Penny, poet and playwright, teaches in the Department of Black Community Education, Research and Development, at the University of Pittsburgh. His recent one-act play *Pain in in My Heart* was featured in *New Plays for the Black Theatre*, (1989, Third World Press, Chicago) edited by Woodie King, Jr.

His recent play production, *Clean Drums*, a full-length play based on Pittsburgh's jazz bebop drummer, Jo Harris, was produced by the Kuntu Repertory Theatre of Pittsburgh (1992), and directed by Dr. Vernell A. Lillie.

JAKE [*To* DALEJEAN]: Good Black, I've been on my own since I was thirteen. A kid out of Lil Rock. When white folks had more respect for dogs and cats then they had for Negroes like us. I learned how to carry the stick early in my life. I've judi-popped with low-life and high-life. I done did Kansas City, Chicago, Memphis, Detroit, Mississippi, New Orleans, Kentucky, Cleveland and God knows where else. I did all there was to do. Did it to men and women and had it done to me. I've sang all of Jimmy Reed's songs in women's ears in every juke joint on Centre Avenue, Wylie Avenue, and this side of West Hell...Ever since I was thirteen, I gone thru life seeing things that I wanted: cars, clothes, houses, dogs, shoes, and yes, oh yes, women. Boo-coo women. Nothing can be without the right woman, and I guess a man wants every fine woman he takes a liking to. But there're so many of them. So many he can't get...I'm fed up. Fed up with not getting what I want. Busting my behind over forty years, eating beans and leftovers...and all those bastards who ain't paid no dues...not one bow dollar...not even one red cent of dues...those who come up after the war's over...who don't know what it be like eating beans without meat...to wear dirty, raggedy, outta style clothes...bastards...who eat fresh vegetables and drink fruit juices...and sleep on waterbeds...with tender hands like some broads...bastards...who don't even wash diapers anymore...they the ones who wound up getting all the goodies in life...Yeah, I'm fed up to my limit.

★

scene from
GOOD BLACK
by Rob Penny

_____

[*Harris's frontroom.* **JANET & JAMES JR.**]

JAMES JR.: [*Seated ams folded.*] Go ahead, Jan. I'm ready.

JANET: First I call you by your free name...Damu...Simba Damu, right?

JAMES JR.: That's Seem-bah. Seem-bah.

JANET: You only have to tell me once.

JAMES JR.: I know, Jan.

JANET: Ready?

JAMES JR.: Yebo!

JANET: That's yes in Zulu. I remember that. Okay. Simba Damu!

JAMES JR.: [*Leaps up in military-style.*] Hapa!. [*He strikes his chest Just above his heart, refolds his ams.*] Appreciate What's been said and if I understand it correctly, the Seven Principles are, One, Umoja (Unity)—To strive for and maintain unity in the family, community, nation and race; Two, Kujichagulia (Self-determination)—To name, define and speak for ourselves instead of being defined and spoken for by others; Three, Ujima (Collective Work and Responsibility)—To build and maintain our community together and to make our brothers and sisters problems our problems and to solve them together; Four, Ujamaa (Cooperative Economics)—To build and maintain our own stores, shops, and other businesses and to profit together from them; Five, Nia (Purpose)—To make as our collective vocation the building and developing of our community in order to restore our people their traditional greatness; Six, Kuumba (Creativity)—To do always as much as we can in the way we can in order to leave our community more beautiful and beneficial than we inherited it; Seven, Imani (Faith)—To believe with all our hearts in our parents, our teachers, our leaders, our people and the righteousness and victory of our struggle. If I've said anything of value and worth, all praises are due Kawaida and Maulana Karenga and all the mistakes have been mine.

JANET: You got 'em all right. Word for word.

JAMES JR.: Asante.

JANET: Boy, it took you a long time to memorize them. I did it in no time.

JAMES JR.: I know you did, Jan. I can remember when you were in McKelvy. They put you two grades ahead of your age. Mom was so happy she cried.

JANET: Do you understand Mom?

JAMES JR.: Not really. I don't understand Phyllis at all. I wish I could talk with her like we can.

JANET: Me too.

JAMES JR.: If we could stop fighting each other.

JANET: Maybe the three of us should do more things together like brother and sisters. Ujima.

JAMES JR.: Jan you're smart. Boy. If Phyllis, you and Mom were to join the National Involvement for Africans...

JANET: James Jr. I'll think about it. I promise.

JAMES JR.: Okay. Good. Now where's my script. I got to go over my lines for the play. You know I'm playing Shaka Zulu. I hope I don't mess up.

JANET: You won't—if you concentrate. I think I'm going to write a play one day.

JAMES JR.: Jan, you can do anything yo want to, you know that. I'm so glad you're my sister.

JANET: And Phyllis?

JAMES JR.: Phyllis too. But she don't listen.

JANET: I know. She doesn't even listen to Mom anymore.

JAMES JR.: Man, I sure hate to see her get strung out in the blood world.

JANET: Phyllis said for us not to answer the phone again. Just in case it's Mom.

JAMES JR.: She's giving out orders now.

JANET: What are you going to do if it rings...?

JAMES JR.: I'm going to my room. If it rings I'm pretending sleep.

JANET: I'm not staying down here by myself.

JAMES JR.: Don't be scared. I locked all the doors and windows. Ah, I'll put a chair under the doorknobs in the kitchen and the frontdoor.

JANET: Then Phyllis won't be able to get in.

JAMES: Good thinking. Yeah and I sleep heavy too.

JANET: I don't. I hear Mom every night when she comes in from work. James Jr., Mom walks real heavy.

JAMES JR.: Probably because she's tired. On her feet eight

hours.

JANET: But Phyllis walks like a cat thru this house. Sometimes I can hear her sneaking pass my room.

JAMES JR.: Where do she be going? To the bathroom?

JANET: Promise you won't tell.

JAMES JR.: I promise.

JANET: To let Darrell in the house.

JAMES JR.: Stupid, stupid.

JANET: James Jr., when Mom talks to herself, does that mean she's going crazy?

JAMES JR.: What do you mean?

JANET: You know how often I have to go to the toilet during the night. Well sometimes when I walk pass Mom's room, I can hear her talking to herself. Out loud. And I know she's in there alone.

JAMES JR.: Yeah, I've caught Mom talking to herself in the kitchen or just walking down the hall upstairs. But I guess she's lonely. All we can do is try not to make her cry anymore than she does. We can't live Mom's life, we don't know how it was for her when she was growing up in Alabama.

JANET: Guess you're right. Maybe she needs an adult around here with her. I'll be glad when I become an adult.

JAMES JR.: Why?

JANET: So I can make enough money to take care of Mom.

JAMES JR.: Look, you go ahead up to your room. I'll double check things down here.

JANET: Can—can I wait for you?

JAMES JR.: Sure.

[**JAMES JR.** & **JANET** *facing in opposite directions.*]

JANET: They say a cat has nine lives...

JAMES JR.: Mom is a good woman...

JANET: God, please don't let Phyllis get in any trouble...

JAMES JR.: I hope Phyllis grows up and be like Mom..

JANET: Watch out for my sister...

JAMES JR.: I'm going to stop calling Phyllis a negro...

JANET: I love my sister...

JAMES JR.: I sure wish Phyllis was home...

JANET: Phyllis, please come home.

JAMES JR.: My fear is for you, Phyllis.

[*Lights Fade Out.*]

★

scene from
THE TENNANT
by Shauneille Perry

Shauneille Perry works in the theatre as a writer, director, and teacher. She is the author of six plays, four musicals, numerous radio and television scripts, articles and essays. Her latest work, a new book for the 1903 Broadway musical *In Dahomey* premiered at Karamu Theatre in 1991. She has directed over 100 plays including the off-Broadway hits *Williams and Walker*, *Sty of the Blind Pig*, *Black Girl*, and *Celebration* which she also authored. She has won three Audelcos, two Cebas, and a Broadcast Media Award. A Fulbright Scholar, she is an Associate Professor and Theatre Director at Lehman College of the City University of New York.

CHARACTERS:
EWW—Elder White Woman [Mrs. Jason]
EBW—Elder Black Woman [Mattie]
YWW—Young White Woman [Rental Agent]
YBW—Young Black Woman [Josephine Amari]

EWW: [*Hustling about.*] My Lord, its almost one o'clock. They'll be here any minute! Mattie! Have you finished making lunch?

EBW: [*Offstage.*] Huh?

EWW: I said, have you finished making lunch yet?

EBW: [*Appearing.*] You just had lunch...I ain't even finished the dishes yet.

EWW: That wasn't lunch, it was brunch.

EBW: I thought it was breakfast.

EWW: Mr. Jason takes breakfast early, I take brunch late.

EBW: Whatever it was it wasn't but an hour ago.

EWW: The point is these people are coming for an interview and I've got to serve them something.

EBW: Better make it dinner 'cause we're into lunch now and I ain't no robot.

EWW: They won't be here that late.

EBW: I hope not.

EWW: Well then...how about coffee or something...can you manage that?

EBW: Now you talking!...With some of them left over Danish from breakfast...uh...uh brunch!

EWW: Fine! Oh Mattie, I'm so nervous...I hate this interviewing...but it's so important to rent to the right people especially in a small house like this with only four apartments.

EBW: Why don't you just let the agent handle it. That's why you got him...

EWW: *Her.* I'm trying a new one this time. Aggressive, pushy sort...but I like her style...She handles a lot of foreign types...European titles and such...

EBW: That what you want?

EWW: They have the money nowadays, Mattie. New money, that is. Old money isn't renting anything. It owns everything.

EBW: Hmmp...Old money. All I know 'bout is *no* money.

EWW: Well for Heaven's sake don't get an attitude today...

EBW: Allright...I'll do my best shuffle.

EWW: Oh Mattie...[*Bell Rings.*] Ah...They're here! You get the coffee, I'll get the door.

EBW: What you want...The sterling or the silverplate?

EWW: [*Happily.*] I'll let you know when I hear the accent.

EBW: I hope it ain't no Spanish...

EWW: Ha Ha!...It wouldn't be...Unless...South American...[*Bell rings again.*] Coming! Scoot Mattie!

YWW: [*Enters brightly.*] Hello Mrs. Jason! I'm just a bit early, I know...

EWW: Well...no, not really...but where is Mrs....uh...uh...

YWW: Amari. She'll be up in a minute. I always arrive before the client...to pave the way so to speak...Life in the U.S. is sometimes confusing to the foreign newcomer...

EWW: I know....I feel the same way abroad....What's her name again?

YWW: ...Amiri.

EWW [*Delicately.*] That's not...Japanese is it?

YWW: Ha, ha...no..no...it's French.

EWW: ...Ahhh!...

[*The bell rings, the Young White Woman gets it quickly...An impeccably stylish young Black woman enters.*]

YWW: Mrs. Jason, may I present Madame Josephine Le Counte Amari from Le Cote Ivoire.

EWW: You said French...

YBW: Je suis Francois Madame, ma pays est le Cote Ivoire...The Ivory Coast...but my English is almost as good as my French..[*Rapidly.*] Now, I understand the apartment is a small one bedroom with a working fireplace, a reasonable kitchen with a window, two closets and is available immediately, n'est pas? Bon, I'll take it!

EWW: [*Still overwhelmed.*] But you haven't even seen it...

YBW: This good woman described it all...

EWW: It's very small...

YBW: No matter...We are only two...mon mari et moi, and his work at the Embassy keeps him so busy he's rarely in...

EWW: ...Embassy?

YWW: Yes...He's a top ranking official..

EWW: ...top ranking...

YWW: ...They're willing to go a lot higher than what you're asking...

EWW: [*Breathless.*] ...I really have to think about it...

YBW: ...a view...it is the same as yours, n'est pas? May I see?

EWW: My God...you didn't say she was BLACK!

YWW: Well....She's foreign Black.

EWW: ...True...

YWW: And French....

EWW: ...Still Black...I don't know...

YWW: She's not Black. She's African.

EWW: Of course....

YWW: I mean Ivory Coast...Senegal...Martinique...Guadaloupe... Haiti...

BOTH: [*A gasp, double take.*] Haiti! Oh No!

YWW: What the Hell....French anyway...

EWW: I've always loved the French....

YWW: She's able to pay Park Avenue rent...if she could rent on Park Avenue that is...

EWW: [*To herself.*]...I want to be liberal...[*Black Woman returns.*]

YBW: [*Effusively.*] C'est marvellieux. A splendid view...

EWW: Would...you both like some...coffee? [*Rings small bell.*]

EBW: [*From offstage.*] Hold your horses!

EWB: [*Embarrassed*] I'll just go and see what the trouble is...[*She goes.*]

YWW: Well...did I pull it off?

EWB: I think so...if we can just seal the deal before she has time to think or consult Mr. Jason...

YBW: ...Or before I talk to Leon...

YWW: Later for Leon! After two years of looking Leon ought to be delighted to get a decent place....if he isn't let him leave and you'll have it all to yourself!

YBW: Oh Norma...I hate playing this game...

YWW: Do you think I like my role any better for God sake? Passing for White and pretending we're not cousins...but...you and your corporate spouse must have a fancy Eastside address...

YBW: ...And I ain't no star

BOTH: Well...

EWW: [*Re-entering Wearily.*] Mattie will be bringing coffee in a minute.

YWW: [*Rising quickly.*] No thanks Mrs. Jason, Madame Amari has to run....Another diplomatic luncheon you know...uh...may I take the papers now to expedite time?

EWW: ...Well...yes...I suppose...I'll just get them from the study...[*She exits as* **YWW** *follows her quickly giving o.k. signal to* **YBW.**]

[*Mattie enters with coffee tray. Puts it down. Looks around, smiles then says:*]

EBW: Y'all get it?

YBW: Yep. Thanks Mom! [*They embrace.*]

★

scene from
TITUS ANDRONICUS
by William Shakespeare

AARON: Touch not the boy, he is of royal blood.

LUCIUS: Too like the sire for ever being good.
First hang the child, that he may see it spawl—
A sight to vex the father's soul withal.
Get me a ladder.
[*A ladder is brought, which Aaron ascends.*]

AARON: Lucius, save the child;
And bear it from me to the empress.
If thou do this, I'll show thee wondrous things
That highly may advantage thee to hear:
If thou wilt not, befall what may befall,
I'll speak no more but 'Vengeance rot you all!'

LUCIUS: Say on, and if it please me which thou speak'st
Thy child shall live, and I will see it nourish'd.

AARON: And if it please thee! Why, assure thee, Lucius,
Twill vex thy soul to hear what I shall speak;
For I must talk of murthers, rapes, and massacres,
Acts of black night, abominable deeds,
Complots of mischief, treason, villainies,
Ruthful to hear, yet piteously perform'd;
And this shall all be buried in my death,
Unless thou swear to me my child shall live.

LUCIUS: Tell on thy mind; I say thy child shall live.

AARON: Swear that he shall, and then I will begin.

LUCIUS: Who should I swear by? Thou believest no god:
That granted, how canst thou believe an oath?

AARON: What if I do not? As, indeed, I do not;

Yet; for I know thou art religious,
And hast a thing within thee called conscience,
With twenty popish tricks and ceremonies,
Which I have seen thee careful to observe,
Therefore I urge thy oath; for that I know
An idiot holds his bauble for a god,
And keeps the oath which by that god he swears,
To that I'll urge him: therefore thou shalt vow
By that same god, what god soe'er it be,
That thou adorest and hast in reverence,
To save my boy, to nourish and bring him up;
Or else I will discover nought to thee.

LUCIUS: Even by my god I swear to thee I will.

AARON: First know thou, I begot him on the empress.

LUCIUS: O most insatiate and luxurious woman!

AARON: Tut, Lucius, this was but a deed of charity
To that which thou shalt hear of me anon.
'Twas her two sons that murdered Bassianus;
They cut thy sister's tongue and ravish'd her,
And cut her hands and trimm'd her as thou sawest.

LUCIUS: O detestable villian! Call'st thou that trimming?

AARON: Why, she was wash'd, and cut, and trimm'd, and 'twas
Trim sport for them which had the doing of it.

LUCIUS: O barbarous beastly villians like thyself!

AARON: Indeed, I was their tutor to instruct them.
That codding spirit had they from their mother,
As sure a card as ever won the set;
That bloody mind I think they learn'd of me,
As true a dog as ever fought at head.
Well, let my deeds be witness of my worth.
I train'd thy brethren to that guileful hole

Where the dead corpse of Bassianus lay;
I wrote the letter that thy father found,
And hid the gold within that letter mentioned,
Confederate with the queen and her two sons:
And what not done, that thou hast cause to rue,
Wherein I had no stroke of mischief in it?
I play'd the cheater for thy father's hand,
And, then I had it, drew myself apart,
And almost broke my heart with extreme laughter.
I pry'd me through the crevice of a wall
When, for his hand, he had his two sons' heads;
Beheld his tears, and laugh'd so heartily
That both mine eyes were rainy like to his:
And when I told the empress of this sport,
She sounded almost at my pleasing tale,
And for my tidings gave me twenty kisses.

FIRST GOTH: What, canst thou say all this, and never blush?

AARON: Ay, like a Black dog, as the saying is.

LUCIUS: Art thou not sorry for these heinous deeds?

AARON: Ay, that I had not done a thousand more.
Even now I curse the day, and yet, I think,
Few come within the compass of my curse,
Wherein I did not some notorious ill:
As kill a man, or else devise his death;
Ravish a maid, or plot the way to do it;
Accuse some innocent, and foreswear myself;
Set deadly enmity between two friends;
Make poor men's cattle break their necks;
Set fire on barns and haystalks in the night,
And bid the owners quench them with their tears.
Oft have I digg'd up dead men from their graves,
And set them upright at their dear friends' door,
Even when their sorrows almost was forgot,
And on their skins, as on the bark of trees,
Have with my knife carved in Roman letters,

'Let not your sorrow die, though I am dead.'
But I have done a thousand dreadful things
As willingly as one would kill a fly,
And nothing grieves me heartily indeed
But that I cannot do ten thousand more.

LUCIUS: Bring down the devil, for he must not die
So sweet a death as hanging presently.

AARON: If there be devils, would I were a devil,
To live and burn in everlasting fire,
So I might have your company in hell,
But to torment you with my bitter tongue!

LUCIUS: Sirs, stop his mouth, and let him speak no more.

★

A scene from
JESSE AND THE GAMES, JESSE OWENS, OLYMPIAD
by Garland Lee Thompson

Garland Lee Thompson, who is currently celebrating thirty five years in the theatre as a playwright, producer, director, actor, Audelco Award-winner, winner of the Washington, D.C. One-Act Play Festival, and founder of the internationally acclaimed, 1989 Obie Award-winning, Frank Silvera Writers' Workshop of New York City. His play, *Papa B On The D Train*, originally presented in 1973 by Woodie King Jr, in the Black Theatre Alliance Festival at the Billie Holiday Theatre in Brooklyn, New York, and later at the BTA Festival in 1976 at the American Place Theatre, is part two of his trilogy of plays, *The Sisyphus Trilogy*. His play, *Jesse And The Games, Jesse Owens, Olympiad*, was first presented in 1983 by the Frank Silvera Writers' Workshop at the former Amphitheatre of the Schomburg Center Library of New York, and was presented by Woodie King Jr. at the Inner City Cultural Center of Los Angeles, during the 1984 Olympic Arts Festival. He is a member of the advisory board of the National Black Theatre Festival, held in Winston-Salem, N.C. in the summer of 1991 and planned the new play presentation series for the summer of 1993. He is currently writing the Frank Silvera Writers' Workshop's documentation, *The Best of The Silvera Years, The History of the American Black Theatre Movement in the Seventies and Eighties*.

CHARACTERS:
> JESSE OWENS, USA Black Olympic track star
> LUTZ LONG, German long jump champion
> RALPH METCALFE, USA Black Olympic track star
> JOSEPH WILLIAMS, a White sports reporter at the 1936 Summer Olympics

[*The lights fade up on* JESSE *and* LUTZ *on the winners stand receiving the roaring approval of the crowd for the long jump championship. Jesse salutes, Lutz gives the German salute.*]

ANNOUNCER: [*Voice-over.*] Owens of the USA, first place for the gold medal in the long broad jump...[*The crowd roars.*] Tajima of Japan, third place for the bronze medal. [*The crowd roars again.*] LUTZ LONG!!! [*Shouting.*] Jazze Owens! Jazze Owenz! [*He freezes.*]

JESSE: Luz Long! Luz Long! The crowd is cheering me. But only I know who they are really cheering! Luz Long! Luz Long! Luz Long! Luz Long! [*He pauses.*] Yet, it isn't Luz who is lifting me into the heavens today! I know who has brought me from the precipice of hell to be able to ascend into the heavens today for this great victory in winning the gold! The gold of Olympia. A permanent placque on the famous wall of the Hall of Fame.

LUTZ LONG: On Berlin's Olympische Sieger! Leichialfletick manner! Our records permanently carved on the hall of fame here in Berlin. Jazze Owenz, and Lutz Long, forever!

JESSE: It wasn't Jesse Owens who really did it! It wasn't anyone who ever ran, or jumped or balanced on that precipice of hell or heaven. No., Luz Long may not know if he believes in God, but God believes in Luz Long! Luz doesn't realize it, but he sure as I am standing here, made Luz his sacred messenger right here in Berlin this week. Hey Luz...[*Calling to* LUTZ, *Jesse continues to face the audience.*] Did I tell you that my mother, bless her poor heart, got so excited during the broad jump trials that she was, unable to walk or talk!

LUTZ LONG: The poor lady, is it true Jazze?

JESSE: Is it true? Luz, she is my best fan, man! Yeah, during a meet which I was competing in recently, my poor momma got so nervous that it was necessary to summon a doctor! She was on the verge of having a stroke from the excitement of me, her son, in the races. And Ruth, my wife, when she received a letter from me in Berlin, she was so overcome with joy that she b rst into tears. Momma, said she cried like baby!

LUTZ LONG: Jazze, I can see the headlines now, Wife Weeps! The wife of Olympic champion Jazze Owenz weeps with joy and the mother states that she has been unable to prepare a meal or do any housework since the Olympics began in Berlin. You are a lucky man Jazze, they all love you!

JESSE: Yeah, they're pulling hard for me! Say, Luz, don't forget to write and keep in touch when it is all over, okay?

LUTZ LONG: You have my word of honor, Jazze, and don't you forget also, my friend.

JESSE: You got it, pal!...*[They shake hands the sound of the crowd roars again and* **RALPH METCALFE** *enters.*] We showed them who is the best of the best of the best...yah, ever hit the black cinders of that pretty little stadium built in Berlintown just right for Jesse, right, and the games! Right Ralph?

RALPH: Right, Brother Jesse, we showed them good! Right from the start with Cornelius Johnson taking the Gold in the high jump, that we came to Berlin "to kick ass and take names!" Dave Albritton took the silver and Johnson having already won the first place, was just waiting around for the results. As soon as "Der Fuehrer" had finished his little greeting of the Finns who won the 10,000 meters, "Der Fuehrer's" flag came down quick, zoom, from the staff above the tribune and his "little German behind" left the stadium, but fast!—Yes he did, as the Lord is my witness...Amid a buzzing of excitment and wonder in the stands! Man, it's all over the papers and radio. Your man, Joseph Williams broke the story first, who did Der Fuehrer smile at and why?...Us, of course, and we know why, need I say more! Shoot man, Jesse, we just blew him, Der Fuehrer, farther out of his cute little box...and clean out of the ball park! Yes we did! And for Marty and Sammy too, and for all of us...and the folks back home! Yeah! Seig Heil to that—indeed. You got that right, Jesse, man! [**LUTZ LONG** *enters and stands on the winners' stand.*] What you say, Lutz? Did we do it?!

LUTZ LONG: Right Ralph! Yes, it is true. I salute you both and myself with the silver medal in the broad jump behind you, Jazze. Olympian, we are champions of Mount Olympia! Born to run, to jump, to prove, to win for all mankind for all times throughout the ages...like the flame of the Olympic torch, burning...

JESSE: Forever! Shining bright! Together forever! [*The sound of*

211

the crowd swells as they all stand again on the winners' stand facing the audience and saluting as **JOSEPH WILLIAMS** *enters and speaks with the music playing 'America the Beautiful'.*]

JOSEPH WILLIAMS: [*Sport reporter.*] There you have it ladies and gentlemen, victory here in Berlin for Jesse Owens, Ralph Metcalfe, Lutz Long and all the rest of the great stars. This Olympics ends today. They have done their work well! Yes, since this moment shall live forever in the hearts and minds of those who are here today...indeed, even the Nazi Aryans are joining thousands of ordinary Germans and sports fans who are standing cheering and applauding in noisy tribune, here in the Olympic Stadium, as Jesse Owens and this great U.S. Team leaves the field. And you sports fans are there. Front row seats for "Jesse and the Games"...Jess Owens, Olympian...The fastest human alive, the world salutes you! This is Joseph Williams, your roving sports reporter, signing off...
[*The lights fade to black.*]

★

scene from
PAPA B ON THE D TRAIN
A New York Subway Play in Two Acts
by Garland Lee Thompson

CHARACTERS:
Papa B/Charlie—Old Black Man—50 to 60 yrs
Carl/Young Man—Young Black Man 20 yrs
Norris/The Drag Queen—Young Black man 20 to 30 yrs
Lambert/The Thief—Young Black man 30 yrs
Isabel/The Young Woman—Young Black woman 20 yrs
Le Noir X—Young Black male playwright 30 yrs
Subway passengers/Dancers—Optional in number

SCENE: The lights comes up on a dingy old subway station.

[*An old tattered Black man,* **PAPA B**, *quietly singing, talking to himself and is rummaging through a large trash can. A young Black man,* **CARL**, *enters. He looks around and up and down the tracks and at the old bag man. He approaches the old man and speaks.*]

CARL, THE YOUNG MAN: Pardon me sir, do you know a good place to die?

PAPA B, THE OLD MAN: Uh, what?

CARL, THE YOUNG MAN: To die...someplace good?

PAPA B, THE OLD MAN: Oh yeah, well, uh, no sonny by, I sure don't, but do you want some pussy?

CARL, THE YOUNG MAN: Pussy! Oh I see...Uh no thanks!

PAPA B, THE OLD MAN: You don't wanta do nothin', do you? You sure now?...I got some real juicy...

CARL, THE YOUNG MAN: No, no!...Man, you don't understand...That's not what I'm into now! Yeah, dig it...the only hole I'm interested in is a big bottom-less one...Oblivion!!!!! Yeah, that's what I'm into!...Can you dig it? I mean let's wrap it up. You know, that lying-down and wrapping-the raggeries-of ones'-rack-about your ass and crashing into sweet dreams bit. You know what I mean...It can't be too deep for you, Pops...I mean, shit man, it can't be that...

PAPA B, THE OLD MAN: Hey, hey, young cat!! I read you, sport! All I asked you was could you handle a "little." And if you can't handle it, well, forget it. You can just blow it out your...

CARL, THE YOUNG MAN: Alright, alright pops, I'm sorry man...Be cool! ...Forget it!...I mean...It's just that I'm pretty up-tight and up to here with the horse-shit, dumb-ass scenes that I've been running into in this freaky-ass life-illusion! Oh, man, what a heavy-ass load!!...I'm cuttin' out baby!! Yeah, can you dig it. I Am splitting...

PAPA B, THE OLD MAN: Alright, alright! Damn! I'm starting to get the picture, kid...Yeah, well, relax now and say, kid....

CARL, THE YOUNG MAN: Yeah, yeah, make it quick pops! I ain't time for jiving!

PAPA B, THE OLD MAN: Okay, okay, Peter Rabbit...But, just do one thing before you go?

CARL, THE YOUNG MAN: Yeah, yeah, what?...

PAPA B, THE OLD MAN: Stay!...[*Laughs.*] Sorry. Don't hit me. I just couldn't resist it, young fellow. I'm an old dude, young sport. I don't get many lead-ins like that much anymore. But, seriously, I mean if that's possible, now! Since killing one's self is such a panic and life ain't such fun. [*Sings.*] "Ray, ray, ray, your boat gently dawns the sun. Merrily, merrily, merrily, life is but a pun!" I Wait don't say it! I know. Out of my skull, right? Right on! But listen and hear me good. [*Pauses.*] Just upstairs, clean, cheap! Be the first on your block to where that last "piece" is coming from!!!! Do your death thing later!

CARL, THE YOUNG MAN: Oh shit, man, it'll be just my luck to catch the clap, or creeping crotch, or something....

PAPA B, THE OLD MAN: Hell, with your schedule, what difference do it make!

CARL, THE YOUNG MAN: You know, you crazy old mother, you might just have a point there.

PAPA B, THE OLD MAN: Yes sir, it really do not matter say the mad-hatter. I ain't justa shuckin' and jivin' Cause my theory is: "Relax, it will all be over someday! Worry not and fear less cause, it is already too late!"

CARL, THE YOUNG MAN: Uh, yeah, uh, well, that's cool, but....

PAPA B, THE OLD MAN: No rest for the wicked and no wicked for the rest!! Know what I mean?

CARL, THE YOUNG MAN: Un, huh, I'm on to it and you. Uh, huh. Well, look, I'll check you...

PAPA B, THE OLD MAN: What you say!! Listen well, child of the earth, to what I say! I am a Black mariner in mourning. I sailed the great white sea, see.

CARL, THE YOUNG MAN: No jive! You lay it on pretty good but....

PAPA B, THE OLD MAN: No bullshit! You bullshit your friends and I'll bullshit mine, but let's not bullshit each other. You see, I cut my teeth on camel shit, cause bullshit was unknown in them days! How 'bout it champ? Won't you camp with me Omar, and let us go over you with a fine toothcomb, Bill baby? That's what they call me, Buffalo-in' Bill!

CARL, THE YOUNG MAN: You think your ass is so smooth that it can slide down the edge of a razor blade without gittin' sliced...Look old man...What I'm trying to get through to your butt is that being on this planet with the MAN is like being afloat on a life-raft with somebody who hates your ass, and you can't stand his. I mean I just can't handle it so I just want to go on and take my "tukus" away and out jack!!

PAPA B, THE OLD MAN: Quiet! Please I, must practice my instrument! [*He strikes a pose*,]

CARL, THE YOUNG MAN: Oh, uh, sorry...What instrument you play, my man?

PAPA B, THE OLD MAN: [*He picks his nose.*] Uni-nose! Nose-phone and bongo-boggers!

CARL, THE YOUNG MAN: Outa-sight Hey...do bogger-woggies...dig it! Like the good old big toe-jam days! Or "Blow It Out Your Nose," by...

PAPA B, THE OLD MAN: Cool it! [*He listens.*] Sheeet...do you believe it, hell..I just got my "calling."

CARL, THE YOUNG MAN: Uh-huh, I just made "first pastor" of the biggest mother congregation in the hold damn city, willie!..What you say, "Rev!" What church?

PAPA B, THE OLD MAN: De A.M.E...on the I.R.T., Broadway line..number One Train. Thank you Jesus! Crowded every Lord's day! Yes sir, "African Massa Epissable," Amen. De Naz, De Lord done giveth and "tukus" away...

★

monologue from
PAPA B ON THE D TRAIN
by Garland Lee Thompson

[CARL, THE BLACK YOUNG MAN *is speaking to Papa B,
the old Black bag man, who lives in the old abandoned 91st Street,
New York Subway station.*]

CARL, THE YOUNG MAN: My scene is THE STAGE, theatre,
Black theatre! The Black act, jack! The Black market! The
thievery of art! Man, you heard 'bout the B.M.T. players, ...huh?
No shit, I'm a show-biz nigger! You go it, jack! The B.M.T.
players!...Black...mo...ther...fuckin'...The...ate...ter...A long-ass
train that just keeps on keepin' on, and gettin' up and down, jack!
Can you come where I'm diggin' from? Dig this number entitled,
"Exit Hollywood." My life-in Hollywood and exit thereof...I
didn't just go away,...I went MAD!...Hatter mad to high yellar, but
independently wealthy for it all...and a painful pane in my mind's
window...with an illusionary mind chronicle in my ass pocket
....Thus, I did not pause, knowing quite well that to do so, was a
fuckin' loss!..Indeed,...a leaping giant became I, cried pretty
niggafus, a petty playwright or wrong, who did write...and left!
[CARL, THE YOUNG MAN *bows and* PAPA B, THE OLD
MAN *applauds*] Yeah, man, the niggers are doin' it! Writin' their
thing down. Taking it to a "Black Place." Truth! Sheeet, man,
didn't you go see, "I'M NEVER ALONE ANYMORE WITH
WHITEY," by Henry Thoreau Kingsley, the third. Or that other
bad piece, "I'S GETS IN YO SMOKE," by the Black queen, Big
Momma Mary-Jo Boo. Or the OOBA award winner, "STOP," by
Gay Montenegro. Sheeet, it really took me out...And oh yeah, my
main man Lambert Beachwood Hollyridge's musical about a
Black Peter Pan called, "PEANUT BUTTER." A dynamite show
baby. Where the hell have you been, jack? And yeah, "THE
YEAR OF THE BLACK RAT," Guy Hay Fat Choy Johnson's
new play is just down the street from here, near wine square. A
boss piece ....[*A Black man dressed in woman's clothes and afro-
wig entersthe subway platform. He faces upstage with his back to*
CARL *and* PAPA B. CARL *notices the new comer, and
approaches the new drag-queen, thinking he is a she. Carl starts*

to recite to her.] Come here pretty momma, let me check out ya hips. [*The drag-queen moves away and* **CARL** *follows.*]
Come here pretty momma and let me check out ya hips. [*The drag-queen tries to avoid* **CARL**.] Oh yeah, sweet thing from the check-out, I moves to the check-in, right? Tight!...Solid...and out of sight! Oh, you know I won't bite. Yeah, come here pretty momma and let me check out ya hips. Y'all think I just wanna cop your sweet field of clover. [*The drag-queen rushes away to the end of the subway platform.*] Sheeet, there she go. Nigger, you gotta git ya program over! [**CARL** *reaches the drag-queen.*] Hey pretty momma, from the git, I don't play that shit! Y'all know my name, Righteous brother is my name. I swear to you baby, I ain't no lick and a promise-jivesucker or no two-timin' dirty motherfucker! What you say! Oh, come here pretty momma, let me check..out..ya..hips..[*He faces "her."*] Hey,...what's happenin?

★

scene from
THE BALLAD OF THE THREE LEGGED MAN
by Edgar Nkosi White

Edgar Nkosi White is a playwright and novelist. He has published over five books of plays as well as four books of fiction. His plays have been performed around the world and broadcast by, among others, the B.B.C. in London. Five of his plays have been produced by Joe Papp at the Public Theatre: *The Lament for Rastafari*, *Les Femmes Noires* (Black Women). His play, *Like Them That Dream*, was performed in England and in New York by the Negro Ensemble. His most recent novel, *The Rising*, was published by Marion Boyars. Two of his plays have been produced by the New Federal Theatre: *The Defence* and *Trinity* under Woodie King.

At present he is working on a production with Ellen Stewart at the Cafe La Mama *Live from Galilee* based on *The Scottsboro Boys*.

CHARACTERS:
> DAVID LEE PORTER, the father.
> RIDCHARD LEE PORTER, the son.
> VICTORIA, the wife and mother.
> RACIMA, the housekeeper.

SCENE: Richard Lee Porter is doing extremely well finally after many years of struggle as an actor. Suddenly one night his father who he has not seen in ten years appears at his door. Richard has worked very hard to seperate himself from his past. He has settled into a new identity. He has nothing to do with anything Black if he can help it. Everyone from his wife to his agent is White, he is therefore anxious to get rid of this ghost as quickly as possible. The father appears in a track suit. The symbol of the play is, in fact, runners, and the way people try to escape from themselves. This scene takes place at the beginning of the play.

[*Urgent sound of doorbell ringing. Light comes up on elderly but physically erect Black man wearing tracksuit. A Spanish woman eventually opens the door to him. She wears a bathrobe and it is evident that she has been sleeping.*]

WOMAN: Yes, what you want?

MAN: Hello, is Mr. Porter at home?

WOMAN: Yes, he's here but they sleeping.

MAN: Yes, well, can you wake him please?

WOMAN: Wake him?...I don't think so, you better come back tomorrow. [*Closing door.*]

MAN: Tell him that it's his father.

WOMAN: His father? Dios Mio. Wait please. Should have stayed in my bed. [*Goes and knocks.*] Senior Porter. Senior Porter.

VOICE: What is it, Racima?

RACIMA: Theres a man at the door who says he's your father.

VOICE: What? Oh shit. What does he want? [*Door opens. He stands in pajamas.*] I've got a shoot in the morning.

RACIMA: You want I should send him away?

RICHARD: No, I know him, he won't leave. All right, I'll be right there...where's my wallet? Jesus, what time is it?

RACIMA: About two o'clock senior.

RICHARD: I'll kill him...[*Gets bathrobe.*] All right you go to bed.

RACIMA: I didn't know what to do. I see this Negro man...

RICHARD: Yes, yes, you go to bed. [*She goes with him to door and stands behind him peering.*] Dad, what do you want?

FATHER: Hi son, how you doing?

RICHARD: How the hell you think I'm doing at two o'clock in the god damn morning?

FATHER: [*Pats him on stomach.*] Putting on a little weight ain't you?

RACIMA: [*Laughing.*] He likes to eat. I cook for them.

RICHARD: Racima, will you go to bed please.

RACIMA: Yes, senior. Good night.

FATHER: Night-night, don't let the bed bugs bite.

RACIMA: Bed bugs? [*She exits.*]

FATHER: Papacito, thats Spanish for...

RICHARD: What the hell are you doing here?

FATHER: Well I was in the neighborhood.

RICHARD: Central Park?

FATHER: Well I was training.

RICHARD: Training for what?

FATHER: The marathon.

RICHARD: You mean you still...?

FATHER: Sure, you didn't think I would quit did you?

RICHARD: At your age?

FATHER: What the hell you mean at my age?

RICHARD: Dad, how old are you?

FATHER: I'm as young as I feel.

RICHARD: Got to be seventy if you a day.

FATHER: Sixty...eight

RICHARD: And you out running around Central Park at two o'clock in the morning.

FATHER: What I got to lose?

RICHARD: Your damn life.

FATHER: You know, an idea came to me. Wouldn't it be nice if my son joined me.

RICHARD: Join you, what you mean join you?

FATHER: I want you to run with me.

RICHARD: Run with you?

FATHER: [*Touching him.*] Yeah, the marathon. You and me.

RICHARD: [*Laughs.*] Are you crazy? You think I want to get a heart attack or something. Things are just starting to happen for me finally. I got me a T.V. show that's a hit. I got some commercials going. A film coming up. You really think I'm going to jeopardize all that for a race?

FATHER: I got this diet plan. You could train with me. Get rid of some of the weight. [*Patting him on belly.*] Soy beans and juice. You'll feel like your flying.

RICHARD: I don't want to fly, I want to sleep. I got an appointment first thing in the morning right, you out of here.

FATHER: We could do it, the two of us together. [**RICHARD**

pushes him towards door.] It would be the first thing we did together besides fight.

RICHARD: Look its been good seeing you. I'm glad your in shape. [Takes out wallet]. Call me some time.

FATHER: What for, you never answer.

RICHARD: I've been busy.

FATHER: Too busy to answer your father?

RICHARD: My father was always too busy to answer me, remember? [*Bedroom door opens and an English woman appears.*]

VICTORIA: I thought I heard voices.

FATHER: Hell, hello there, is this my daughter-in-law?

RICHARD: Everything's fine Victoria, you go back to bed.

VICTORIA: [*To father.*] I beg your pardon?

FATHER: I'm Richard's father. [*Walking toward her.*] If I waited on him to introduce us I'd be dead.

RICHARD: Okay Victoria, this is dad, he was just leaving.

FATHER: Its starting to rain.

RICHARD: [*Taking out money.*] Here, take a taxi.

VICTORIA: Pleased to meet you Mr. Porter, I've often wondered where Richard came from.

FATHER: Seed of my seed and fruit of my fruit. Or is it loins, yep, loins. David Lee Porter at your service. [*Reaches around* **RICHARD** *and shakes her hand.*]

VICTORIA: How do you do.

FATHER: Hot damn, and she's British too.
RICHARD: Goodnight, Dad.

VICTORIA: You can't just send him out into the rain.

RICHARD: He comes with rain.

VICTORIA: Well at least call a taxi for him.

RICHARD: [*Runs to phone.*] Where you going, Dad?

FATHER: I don't know, son.

RICHARD: Where do you live?

FATHER: In the dessert.

RICHARD: [*Slams down phone.*] Look, I don't have any more time for your games. You don't live in no damn dessert. Where you staying?

VICTORIA: Perhaps your father would like a bit of coffee or something?

RICHARD: I don't care what....

FATHER: Coffee is bad for you before a race. A little herb tea would be nice though.

VICTORIA: Why certainly, and I have some excellent biscuits. Tell me how are you with Marmalade jam?

FATHER: Lady, I been in jams all my life.

VICTORIA: How about you Richard?

RICHARD: Yeah, fine. You go make something.

VICTORIA: Good, now just sit down and relax. [*To father.*] What's that around I your neck?

FATHER: A medallion. I run the marathon.

VICTORIA: How fascinating.

FATHER: I'm trying to get my son to run with me.

VICTORIA: [*Laughing.*] Richard? That would be interesting.

RICHARD: Weren't you making tea or something?

VICTORIA: Won't be a moment. [*She exits.*]

RICHARD: Okay you, seed of my seed and fruit of my loins, my ass. You're out of here, now. Here take this money. You stop anything that's moving and get in it.

FATHER: Its raining.

RICHARD: Here, take the umbrella.

FATHER: They might think I'm going to mug them. What about my tea?

RICHARD: That's all right, I'll apologize for you.

FATHER: [*Throwing down umbrella.*] No, I'm not leaving.

RICHARD: Oh, you leaving all right. If I've got to drop you from this window, you're leaving.

FATHER: When was the last time that we sat and talked together, Richard?

RICHARD: It doesn't matter, the truth is we don't have a damn thing to talk about.

FATHER: What are you so scared of son?

RICHARD: Scared of? Nothing. You're just an embarrassment to me that's all. Can you understand that? When the hell are you going to grow up? You're still running around like some damn kid.

FATHER: At least I'm alive. You, were always an old man.

RICHARD: Sure, why shouldn't you be alive. You never faced any responsibilities in your whole life. Thats why mom is dead and you're still here. Whenever things get hard you run. I guess you should be pretty good at it by now.

FATHER: You still holding that against me?

RICHARD: You think I was just going to forget? You dumped us and went off to become a star, right?

FATHER: And so thats why maybe you're the star. So why hate me?

RICHARD: So now you want to take the credit for my success. Let me tell you something. It had nothing to do with you. I just know one thing. if I hadn't made it you wouldn't even spit on me.

FATHER: Look, I'm a new man now, God forgave me, why can't you?

RICHARD: Because God didn't need you, I did. Thats why.

VICTORIA: [*Entering with tray.*] Tea is ready.

RICHARD: He doesn't have time. He's leaving.

VICTORIA: [*Aside.*] Richard, If anything were to happen to him tonight, would you ever be able to forgive yourself?

RICHARD: Yes, very easily.

VICTORIA: Well I might not. [*Gives him meaningful look.*]

RICHARD: All right, all right. You can sleep here on the couch, but tomorrow I want you out, you understand?

FATHER: [*Runs to couch and sits. Takes up cup of tea.*] Thank you.

RICHARD: I got to get some sleep.

FATHER: Good night my son.

RICHARD: Yeah...sure. Good night...my father.

[*Darkness. Scene.*]

★

monologue from
THE BALLAD OF THE THREE LEGGED MAN
by Edgar Nkosi White

SCENE: The FATHER wakes up in the living-room of his son's house. He finds himself alone. He does a few streaches and rejoices in his good fortune. He takes up the small knap-sack that he carries and withdraws a bag of peanuts.

TIME: Later on the same day as the preceding scene.

FATHER: Thank you Jesus. Well, might as well heat up these nuts, start my day right. [*He runs off stage to kitchen area and then returns.*] The boy living good. [*He looks about room and sees a picture of his late wife,* THELMA, *on the table. Examines photograph and laughs to himself.*] Well Thelma, he's got your picture up, he don't have none of me. I guess you win. You were a good woman Thelma, had that pretty Indian hair, part Cherokee, part angel. Too bad we could never see eye-to-eye. You were always trying to change me and I was always busy running. Why Thelma? [*Sits down.*] How could two people who were so much in love, spend so much time fighting? You knew who I was first time that you met me. Told you I wanted to be on stage, thats what I was born to do. You said: "All Right, All Right." Then we got married and the first thing you wanted me to do was get a job in the post office. Me, David Lee Porter. Working for some post office, no way that was go work. Then the baby came, I ran. I'm not go lie, can't lie, I ran like a river. Guess I been running most all my life. Running from the South, running from Death, running from myself I guess. Hard for a man to run on three legs. Wherever my Johnson pointed I'd follow. [*He laughs.*] Had me tripping over myself, damn near couldn't get out of my own way. [*Pause.*] Well, I seen the light. First you play and then you pay. The only good thing that ever happened to me was you and the boy. He's famous now. I'm glad for him. He made it, I didn't. Don't make any sense to be jealous of your own son. Me, I'm glad for him. Bible says, old men dream dreams and young men shall see visions. Well I'm still seeing visions. He thinks that all I want from him is his money. As if money could save somebody. It's his love I want, but now he's the one that's running. Running too fast to hear my love. But Thelma, I know something now. I know that he needs me more than he ever did. He needs me to tell him things about the other side of the river. He's trying to lose himself in their world and it won't work. You can run but you can't hide. When he see's my face, it reminds him of his own. Thats why he needs me. [*Sudden sound of explosion off-stage.*] What the hell was that?

RACIMA: [*Entering angrily.*] Senior, did you put something in the micro-wave?

FATHER: Oh Lord....[*Smiles sheepishly.*] May I have one phone call to my lawyer?

[*Darkness.*]

★

ONE ON ONE
BEST MONOLOGUES FOR THE 90'S
Edited by Jack Temchin

You have finally met your match in Jack Temchin's new collection, *One on One*. Somewhere among the 150 monologues Temchin has recruited, a voice may beckon to you—strange and alluring—waiting for your own voice to give it presence on stage.

"The sad truth about most monologue books," says Temchin, "is that they don't give actors enough credit. I've compiled my book for serious actors with a passionate appetite for the unknown."

Among the selections:
David Mamer OLEANNA
Richard Greenberg THE AMERICAN PLAN
Brian Friel DANCING AT LUGHNASA
John Patrick Shanley THE BIG FUNK
Terrence McNally LIPS TOGETHER, TEETH APART
Neil Simon LOST IN YONKERS
David Hirson LA BETE
Herb Gardner CONVERSATIONS
WITH MY FATHER
Ariel Dorfman DEATH AND THE MAIDEN
Alan Ayckborn A SMALL FAMILY BUSINESS

$7.95 • paper
MEN: ISBN: 1-55783-151-3 • WOMEN: ISBN: 1-55783152-1

APPLAUSE

A PERFORMER PREPARES

A GUIDE TO SONG PREPARATION FOR ACTORS, SINGERS AND DANCERS

by David Craig

A PERFORMER PREPARES is a class act magically transformed to the printed page. It's a 13-part Master-class on how to perform, on any stage from bleak rehearsal room to the Palace Theater. The class covers the basic Broadway song numbers, from Show Ballad to Showstopper. With precise, logical steps and dynamic and enteraining dialogues between himself and his students, Craig takes anyone with the desire to shine from an audition to final curtain call. These lessons on the page recreate as closely as possible the unique interpersonal dynamic of Craig's legendary coaching encounters in New York and Los Angeles.

$21.95 cloth
ISBN: 1-55783-133-5

🐾 **APPLAUSE** 🐾

MICHAEL CHEKHOV:
ON THEATER AND THE ART OF ACTING
The Six Hour Master Class
Four 90-minute Audio Cassettes
by Michael Chekhov

edited with a 48-page course guide
by Mala Powers

AN AUDIO TREASURE!

Join the legendary teacher/director, heralded as Russia's greatest actor, for a six hour master class on the fundamentals of the Chekhov technique. Among the features:

- The Art of Characterization
- Short Cuts to Role Preparation
- How to Awaken Artistic Feelings and Emotions
- Avoiding Monotony in Performance
- Overcoming Inhibitions and Building Self-Confidence
- Psycho-physical Exercises
- Development of the Ensemble Spirit

$49.95 X
ISBN: 1-55783-117-3

APPLAUSE

SPEAK WITH DISTINCTION

BY EDITH SKINNER

Revised with new material compiled by Timothy Monich and Lilene Mansell

"Edith Skinner's book is the **BEST BOOK ON SPEECH THAT I HAVE EVER ENCOUNTERED.** It was my primer in school and it is my reference book now. To the classical actor, or for that matter any actor who wishes to be understood, this method is a sure guide."

—**Kevin Kline**

"Edith Skinner **CHANGED THE SOUND OF THE AMERICAN THEATRE** and as a director in the classical repertory, I am deeply grateful to her."

—**Michael Kahn**, Artistic Director, Shakespeare Theater at the Folger

"Speak with Distinction is **THE SINGLE MOST IMPORTANT WORK ON THE ACTOR'S CRAFT** of stage speech. Edith Skinner's work must be an indispensable source book for all who aspire to act."

—**Earle Gister**, Yale School of Drama

$34.95X
ISBN: 1-55783-047-9

APPLAUSE

THE THEATRE OF BLACK AMERICANS

Edited by Errol Hill

From the origins of the Negro spiritual and the birth of the Harlem Renaissance to the emergence of a national Black theatre movement, *The Theatre of Black Americans* offers a penetrating look at a Black art form that has exploded into an American cultural institution. Among the essays:

Some African Influences on the Afro-American Theatre
James Hatch

Notes on Ritual in the New Black Theatre
Shelby Steele

The Lafayette Players
Sister M. Francesca Thompson, O.S.F.

The Role of Blacks in the Federal Theatre, 1935-1939
Ronald Ross

$15.95 • paper
ISBN: 0-936839-27-9

BLACK HEROES

SEVEN PLAYS
Edited, with an introduction, by Errol Hill

Some of America's most outstanding playwrights of the last two centuries have catapulted the lives of legendary black men and women out of the history books and onto the stage. Errol Hill has collected the most resonant of these powerful examples in *Black Heroes* where we meet Nat Turner, Frederick Douglass, Harriet Tubman, Martin Luther King, Paul Robeson, Marcus Garvey and Jean Jacques Dessaline.

Here for the first time in one volume are plays—many of which have been unavailable for decades—which pronounce a Black American struggle for freedom, advancement and equality from the days of slavery to the era of civil rights. The full scope of their dramas becomes a *tableau vivante* of black history.

EMPEROR OF HAITI Langston Hughes
NAT TURNER Randolph Edmonds
HARRIET TUBMAN May Miller
IN SPLENDID ERROR William Branch
I, MARCUS GARVEY Edgar White
PAUL ROBESON Philip Hayes Dean
ROADS OF THE MOUNTAIN TOP Ron Milner

$12.95 • paper
ISBN: 1-55783-027-4

🐾APPLAUSE🐾

THE CRAFTSMEN OF DIONYSUS

AN APPROACH TO ACTING
NEW AND REVISED
WITH A NEW CHAPTER ON
AUDITIONING

by Jerome Rockwood

"ROCKWOOD REALLY TAUGHT ME HOW TO ACT—WHAT IT WAS ABOUT, AND WHAT IT WAS NOT ABOUT."
—Bruce Willis

"THE BEST ACTING TEXTBOOK ON THE MARKET TODAY."
—Professor Larry Clark
University Of Missouri

"I WISH I HAD READ IT LONG AGO!"
—Burgess Meredith

HIGHLIGHTS:
Stage Geography • Marking on the Script
Relax! • Sense Memory • Justification
Improvisation • Physicalization • Props
Standard Stage Speech • Dialects and Accents
Style • Movement in Period Plays
Blocking • Naturalism rs. Realism

$17.95 • paper
ISBN: 1-55783-155-6

CREATING A CHARACTER:
A Physical Approach to Acting
by Moni Yakim with Muriel Broadman

"Moni Yakim's techniques to attain characterization have been outstandingly successful in bringing out of his students emotional depth to enrich whatever they do on stage. [He] is an inspired teacher. His ideas and practices, which the book details, make it required reading for every serious student of the theatre."
—from the foreword by Stella Adler

"So often actors forget that there are bodies attached to their character's heads. Through Moni Yakim's technique I learned to develop the physical life of a character, lifting the character off the page and into reality."
—Patti Lupone

"Moni Yakim's teaching awakens the actor's senses and tunes the actor's physicality to a degree of self-expression beyond the merely naturalistic and into the larger realms of imagination and poetry."
—Kevin Kline

paper • ISBN: 1-55783-161-0

APPLAUSE

SHAKESPEARE'S PLAYS IN PERFORMANCE
by John Russell Brown

In this volume, John Russell Brown snatches Shakespeare from the clutches of dusty academics and thrusts him centerstage where he belongs—in performance.

Brown's thorough analysis of the theatrical experience of Shakespeare forcibly demonstrates how the text is brought to life: awakened, colored, emphasized, and extended by actors and audiences, designers and directors.

"A knowledge of what precisely can and should happen when a play is performed is, for me, the essential first step towards an understanding of Shakespeare."
—*from the Introduction by John Russell Brown*

paper•ISBN 1-55783-136-X•

APPLAUSE

SHAKESCENES: SHAKESPEARE FOR TWO

The Shakespeare Scenebook

EDITED AND WITH AN INTRODUCTION
BY JOHN RUSSELL BROWN

Thirty-five scenes are presented in newly edited texts, with notes which clarify meanings, topical references, puns, ambiguities, etc. Each scene has been chosen for its independent life requiring only the simplest of stage properties and the barest of spaces. A brief description of characters and situation prefaces each scene and is followed by a commentary which discusses its major acting challenges and opportunities.

paper ▌ ISBN 1-55783-049-5

APPLAUSE

MONOLOGUE WORKSHOP

From Search to Discovery
in Audition and Performance

by Jack Poggi

To those for whom the monologue has always been
synonymous with terror, *The Monologue Workshop* will
prove an indispensable ally. Jack Poggi's new book answers
the long-felt need among actors for top-notch guidance in
finding, rehearsing and performing monologues. For those
who find themselves groping for speech just hours before
their "big break," this book is their guide to salvation.

The Monologue Workshop supplies the tools to discover
new pieces before they become over-familiar, excavate
older material that has been neglected, and adapt material
from non-dramatic sources (novels, short stories, letters,
diaries, autobiographies, even newspaper columns). There
are also chapters on writing original monologues and
creating solo performances in the style of Lily Tomlin and
Eric Bogosian.

Besides the wealth of practical advice he offers, Poggi
transforms the monologue experience from a terrifying
ordeal into an exhilarating opportunity. Jack Poggi, as
many working actors will attest, is the actor's partner in a
process they had always thought was without one.

paper•ISBN 1-55783-031-2

❤️APPLAUSE❤️

DIRECTING THE ACTION

ACTING AND DIRECTING IN CONTEMPORARY THEATRE
by Charles Marowitz

"An energizing, uplifting work...Reading Morowitz on theatre is like reading heroic fiction in an age without heroes."
— *Los Angeles Weekly*

"A cogent and incisive collection of ideas, well formulated and clearly set forth; an important contribution on directing in postmodern theatre."
— *Choice*

"Consistently thought provoking...Sure to be controversial."
— *Library Journal*

"Stimulating, provocative, sometimes irascible, but always courageous."
— Robert Lewis

$12.95 . Paper
ISBN: 1-55783-072-X

APPLAUSE

MICHAEL CAINE
ACTING IN FILM

An Actor's Take on Movie Making

Academy Award winning actor Michael Caine, internationally acclaimed for his talented performances in movies for over 25 years, reveals secrets for success on screen. Acting in Film is also available on video (the BBC Master Class).

"Michael Caine knows the territory...Acting in Film is wonderful reading , even for those who would not dream of playing 'Lets Pretend' in front of a camera. Caine's guidance, aimed at novices still ddreaming of the big break, can also give hardened critics fresh insights to what it is they're seeing up there on the screen..."
        –Charles Champlin, LOS ANGELES TIMES

BOOK/PAPER: $8.95 • ISBN: 1-55783-124-6
VIDEO: $49.95 • ISBN: 1-55783-034-7

APPLAUSE

SOLO!
The Best Monologues of the 80's
Edited by Michael Earley and Philippa Keil

Over 150 speeches in two volumes (MEN and WOMEN) from the best American and British plays of the 1980's have been selected with the actor's needs in mind. Each volume boasts work from such top dramatists as Sam Shepard, David Mamet, Beth Henley, Marsha Norman, Lanford Wilson, Emily Mann, Christopher Durang, Harold Pinter, Caryl Churchill, David Hare, and Simon Gray. With notes on character, context and approach accompanying each piece, SOLO! takes the mystery out of the audition process and replaces it with confidence and poise.

An invaluable resource entitled *Your 60 Seconds of Fame* guides the actor through the art, business and science of monologue performance. After grasping the demands of the monologue form, the actor is ready to meet the casting director and his or her demands before . . . the dreaded "Next!" *Your 60 Seconds of Fame* covers the terrain from monologue selection through performance.

paper • MEN: ISBN 0-936839-65-1 • WOMEN: ISBN 0-936839-66-X

🐾APPLAUSE🐾

SOLILOQUY!
The Shakespeare Monologues
Edited by Michael Earley and Philippa Keil

At last, over 175 of Shakespeare's finest and most performable monologues taken from all 37 plays are here in two easy-to-use volumes (MEN and WOMEN). Selections travel the entire spectrum of the great dramatist's vision, from comedies and romances to tragedies, pathos and histories.

"SOLILOQUY is an excellent and comprehensive collection of Shakespeare's speeches. Not only are the monologues wide-ranging and varied, but they are superbly annotated. Each volume is prefaced by an informative and reassuring introduction, which explains the signals and signposts by which Shakespeare helps the actor on his journey through the text. It includes a very good explanation of blank verse, with excellent examples of irregularities which are specifically related to character and acting intentions. These two books are a must for any actor in search of a 'classical' audition piece."

ELIZABETH SMITH
Head of Voice & Speech
The Juilliard School

paper • MEN: ISBN 0-936839-78-3 • WOMEN: ISBN 0-936839-79-1

❤️APPLAUSE❤️

CPSIA information can be obtained
at www.ICGtesting.com
Printed in the USA
LVHW082339050920
665203LV00010B/200

9 781557 831743